The Werewolf's Guide to Life

The Werewolf's Guide to Life

A MANUAL FOR THE NEWLY BITTEN

Ritch Duncan and Bob Powers

Illustrations by Emily Flake

Broadway Books
NEW YORK

PUBLISHED BY BROADWAY BOOKS

Published in the United States by Broadway Books,
an imprint of the Crown Publishing Group,
a division of Random House, Inc., New York.

www.crownpublishing.com

BROADWAY BOOKS and its logo, a letter B bisected
on the diagonal, are trademarks of Random House, Inc.

Library of Congress Cataloging-in-Publication Data
Duncan, Ritch.
The werewolf's guide to life : a manual for the newly bitten /
by Ritch Duncan and Bob Powers.—1st ed.
p. cm.
Includes bibliographical references.
ISBN 978-0-7679-3193-9
1. Werewolves—Humor. I. Powers, Bob, 1973– II. Title.

PN6231.W39D86 2009
818'.607—dc22
2009007512

PRINTED IN THE UNITED STATES OF AMERICA

Book design by Elizabeth Rendfleisch

1   3   5   7   9   10   8   6   4   2

First Edition

To all those living with lycanthropy, this one's for you.

Remember, take it one Moon at a time.

CONTENTS

PART ONE
SAY HELLO TO A BRAND-NEW YOU

---

1. The Basics   3

What is lycanthropy?

2. How to Determine If You Are Really a Werewolf   9

The early symptoms of lycanthropy; how you can know if what bit you was actually a werewolf

3. The Stages of Lycanthropy   19

The five stages of lycanthrope life; lifespan versus longevity; what happens when a werewolf dies

4. Purebloods   29

Lycanthropes who are born with the condition; how they differ from the bitten; parenting tips for raising a pureblood

PART TWO

LIVING, LOVING, AND LEARNING . . . WITH LYCANTHROPY

PART THREE

KEEPING SECRET, KEEPING SAFE, STAYING ALIVE

READ THIS FIRST

1. Werewolves are real.

2. If you have been bitten by a werewolf and survived the attack YOU WILL TRANSFORM INTO A WERE-WOLF. Your transformations will occur on the evening of the full moon, as well as the evenings immediately before and after the full moon (waxing and waning). These are popularly called your "Moons." The first transformation will happen roughly a month from the date of your attack. To be clear, if the full moon falls on the fifteenth, you will transform into something very, very dangerous on the evenings of the fourteenth, the fifteenth, and the sixteenth.

3. IF THERE IS A FULL MOON APPROACHING AND YOU HAVE EVEN THE SMALLEST SUSPI-CION THAT YOU HAVE BEEN BITTEN BY A WEREWOLF, TURN TO CHAPTER 5, "TIPS ON YOUR FIRST TRANSFORMATION," IMMEDI-ATELY.

4. If you do not know when the next full moon will be, FIND OUT RIGHT NOW by checking the appendix at the back of the book. If you are reading this after December 2011, learn how to determine the date of the next full moon in Chapter 6, "When It Will Happen and What It Will Feel Like," or check online at www.werewolfguidetolife.com.

5. The majority of lycanthropes who do not have access to the information in this book die during or shortly after their first transformations. Causes of death are generally heart failure, gunshot wounds, exposure, drowning, or suicide.

6. The bulk of the information in this book was originally circulated in the form of xeroxed, handwritten copies of the collected writings, observations, and oral histories of people who have both lived (and died) with lycanthropy. That information has been supplemented via interviews with lycanthropes and those whose lives have been touched by lycanthropy.

7. This book was created to save human lives, including yours.

8. Hollywood horror movies are not to be used as guides to living with lycanthropy. Their goal is not to educate, but to entertain. As a result, they are largely ignorant of the realities of the condition.

9. Ignorance creates monsters; lycanthropy does not.

10. You are not a monster.

Notes on the Text

NAMES AND IDENTIFYING DETAILS

Where lycanthropes and their loved ones are identified by their full names or other identifying details, those names and details have been changed to protect the individuals from those who might do them harm.

TESTIMONIALS

The introductory paragraphs of each chapter are firsthand accounts of people who are living with lycanthropy, who have a loved one who is a werewolf, or whose lives have been touched profoundly by the condition in some other manner. They are excerpts from much longer interviews conducted by the authors while researching this book. The authors thank these brave individuals for sharing their experiences so that future lycanthropes might learn from them. We also thank them for trusting that their anonymity would not be compromised, and we have gone to great lengths to make sure their identities remain hidden.

TRUE LEGENDS?

These text inserts are taken from stories that have been passed down from werewolf to werewolf over the years. We cannot be sure of their veracity, but even if they turn out to be false, we believe they are still helpful either as allegories or coping mechanisms. These legends have persisted for a reason.

USE OF THE MALE PRONOUN

In many cases throughout the book we rely on the use of the male pronoun "he" when speaking of a hypothetical lycanthrope. This is done solely to aid the readability of the text and should not be seen as confirmation of the myth that lycanthropes are always male. Any human being can become a werewolf, regardless of gender or race.

USE OF THE TERMS "WEREWOLVES," "LYCANTHROPES," AND "NON-LYCS"

Throughout the text we use the terms "lycanthrope" and "werewolf" interchangeably. It is a commonly accepted colloquialism among lycanthropes to refer to themselves as "werewolves," and our text reflects this.

We have tried to refer to non-lycanthropes as simply "non-lycs" rather than "humans," since lycanthropes are no less human than non-lycs. Further, in many traditional texts on lycanthropy, the werewolf's two states are divided into the "human" state and the "wolf" state. We believe that both of these states are experienced by the same human being, and so have tried to avoid referring to one state as more human than the other. To this end, we have made a point of signifying the lycanthrope's pre-transformation state as his "dormant" state and his post-transformation, wolf-like state as his "wild" state.

So You've Been Bitten

Introduction

Welcome to *The Werewolf's Guide to Life*, the definitive manual for the recently bitten lycanthrope. If a werewolf has recently attacked you, or you've already transformed into a werewolf, we urge a thorough reading of this text.

Thousands of werewolves living in the twenty-first century have jobs, families, and obligations. They are artists, businesspeople, and scholars; Democrats, Republicans, and Independents. They have backyard barbecues and home gardens, and they celebrate holidays from Easter to Rosh Hashanah to Ramadan.

Unlike the rest of society, werewolves happen to have a condition that, three times a month, causes their bodies to almost double in size, triple in strength and agility, grow a thick mass of tightly woven fur, and transform from an unremarkable human being into a savage, wild animal resembling (but distinctly different from) a wolf, whose behavior patterns are generally dictated by voracious hunger and rage. There is no known cure for this condition because, strictly speaking, it is not a disease. With care and discipline, it is manageable.

This book is written primarily for the recently bitten (Stage

1) lycanthrope. This is a person who is scared, confused, and unable to process what is happening to him. The ignorance of Stage 1 lycanthropes makes them a danger to themselves, general society, and the community of well-adjusted, nonviolent werewolves who have found themselves persecuted as a result of the rampages of the terrified, uneducated few. If we reach just one of these newly bitten werewolves and are able to save his life and, by proxy, the lives of his neighbors and loved ones, we will have achieved our goal. This is not a guide to learn how to fight off a werewolf, and this is not a guide to learn how to become a werewolf. It is a guide to help newly bitten werewolves learn how to retain their humanity.

So if you are one of these recently bitten people, congratulations on your decision to read this far—it very well may have saved your life. What we are presenting to you is a workable road map that will allow you to come to grips with the realities of your condition, design an ethical life for yourself that can be lived to the fullest, and avoid premature death, killing the innocent, or passing your condition to another through violent attack. This book includes everything from short-term survival and transformation techniques to long-term guidance, including diet, wellness (both physical and mental), living arrangements and environments, vocations, dating, sex, love, and child-rearing.

If you have any interest in staying alive, keep reading.

—The authors
September 2009

PART ONE

SAY HELLO TO
A BRAND-NEW YOU

CHAPTER ONE

The Basics

It was a nice night for a walk in the park. Bright. Big moon. Out by the picnic area, I heard this deep, low growling. Scared the hell out of me. Then I heard it circling. Rustling in the bushes. Moving around behind me. I began to think I was in real trouble. When I heard the howl, I knew it. As it exploded out of the bushes at me, I thought two things: It was a rabid animal, and I was done for. Wrong on both counts. We smashed straight through the picnic table, shattering it. I was found the next morning, barely alive, with a dead, naked man, impaled on a shard of the broken table, next to me. I've come around to believing that I was lucky. I didn't always feel that way.

—Marty H., Political Consultant
Age: 34, Lyc age: 10

GETTING STARTED

If you've been bitten by a werewolf or know someone who has been bitten, you probably have a head full of some pretty weird and wild questions. This section will go over the basics of what lycanthropy is all about.

WHAT IS LYCANTHROPY?

Lycanthropy is a biological condition wherein you undergo a cyclical physical transformation, experiencing sudden and drastic growth in all parts of your body until you appear to have been turned into a creature that is half-human/half-wolf. Those who have this condition are called "lycanthropes" or "werewolves." When you undergo this change you experience rapid hair growth; your teeth turn into large fangs and your fingernails grow into long sharp claws; and your body increases in height, girth, and strength, with longer limbs, a more pronounced brow, and in some cases, an extended snout. During the transformation, your mental state experiences a rapid deterioration, eroding all of your higher faculties until your mind is that of a bloodthirsty predator. You will become hungry for flesh and will maul and feed on animals or humans, given the chance. In your "wild" state you are extremely dangerous and hard to control. You remain in your wild state for approximately eight hours before you transform back to your normal or "dormant" state.

WHEN IT HAPPENS

You will experience a transformation three nights out of the month, on the evening of the full moon and the evenings before and after, when the full moon waxes and wanes. These nights are commonly referred to as your "Moons," and the monthly trio of Moons is referred to as your "Moon Set." On the morning following each transformation, you will wake up in your dormant state again, usually with little to no memory of the events of the previous night.

HOW ONE BECOMES A WEREWOLF

You can become a werewolf either by being born to a lycanthrope father or by having a werewolf's blood or fluids introduced into your bloodstream, usually through a bite. The fluids must enter your bloodstream while the werewolf is in his wild state. If you are bitten by a werewolf in his dormant state, or if the fluids of a werewolf are introduced into your bloodstream outside of a transformation day, you will not become a werewolf.

HOW IT HAPPENS

The blood and saliva of werewolves contain a contagion that acts upon the pituitary gland. After you've been attacked, this contagion travels through your bloodstream and causes your pituitary gland to release a rare and normally dormant thyroid-stimulating hormone called lycantropin. Lycantropin acts upon the thyroid and other glands and organs to stimulate growth at a rapid rate, first by causing a breakdown of body structures and then by swift cellular regeneration and reproduction. This hormonal process makes the body grow to nearly twice its normal size and stimulates the hunger and rage receptors in the brain to such an extreme degree that you begin to behave like a starved, wild animal. The process continues for eight to twelve hours until the body counteracts the change and triggers another cellular breakdown, changing your physiognomy back to your dormant state.

For purebloods, lycanthropes who are born to a lycanthrope father, the pituitary gland is preprogrammed to automatically release the lycantropin hormone during Moon Sets after the pureblood reaches puberty.

WHO CAN BECOME A LYCANTHROPE

Any human being, male or female, regardless of race or background, can become a lycanthrope. However, the condition

---

IS THERE A PROCEDURE TO PREVENT THE PITUITARY GLAND FROM RELEASING THE LYCANTROPIN HORMONE?

People who have been recently bitten or lycanthrope parents of pureblood children might seek a surgical procedure to inhibit the release of lycantropin. There is no such procedure that we know of, but were there such a procedure we would oppose its practice. Disabling or manipulating the pituitary gland to inhibit thyroid function is an act of mutilation that would impair the body's natural development and drastically alter its overall chemistry. Were such a procedure performed on a child, it would prevent that child from going through puberty and subject him to a life far worse than that of a pureblood lycanthrope. You might wish that your child were like all of the other non-lycs, but impairing physical development will achieve the very opposite effect. You would be intentionally handicapping your child and stunting his growth.

---

will not become active until you reach the age at which puberty begins. Nonhumans (animals) cannot contract lycanthropy.

WHY IS LYCANTHROPY TIED TO THE PHASES OF THE MOON?

The lycantropin hormone is released in measured doses throughout the month, hitting its peak after approximately twenty-nine days. During the first month, you will notice several changes in your body: hair growth, fingernail growth, and increased strength. Much more is happening internally, including a dramatic spike in the iron levels in your blood. The increase in iron changes the magnetic polarity of your chemical makeup, causing you to be far more sensitive to the phases of the moon. In the way that the ocean hits high tide at full moon, your body experiences a "high tide" of its own, triggering a sudden, massive surge of lycantropin to instigate your change.

IS THERE A CURE?

No, because lycanthropy is not a disease. It is a process involving the release of a hormone that is already present in the body.

IS IT POSSIBLE TO HAVE THIS CONDITION AND LEAD ANYTHING RESEMBLING A NORMAL LIFE?

Absolutely. Keep reading this book to find out how.

CHAPTER TWO

How to Determine If
You Are Really a Werewolf

My first month wasn't scary, just lonely. I knew something wasn't right. I couldn't explain what was happening to me. I actually thought my Propecia had gone out of whack. But I knew the thing that attacked me wasn't what the police said. They said it was a bear. In a suburb of Atlanta.

The second month though, that was scary. Once I got through my first changes, and I realized I had a month to just wait to change again, nothing was more terrifying. At least I didn't need the Propecia no more.

—Joseph H., Physical Therapist
Age: 33, Lyc age: 6

AM I REALLY A WEREWOLF?

If you suspect that a werewolf has bitten you, if it's been less than a month since the attack, and if you have not yet transformed into a werewolf, this is the big question. While it might be comforting to ignore the inexplicable signs, avoidance of this issue can be deadly. If you were bitten by a werewolf, you contracted lycanthropy the instant the attacking werewolf's saliva entered your bloodstream, and as such, there are numerous ways to detect your condition long before your first Moon.

Don't wait. Investigate!

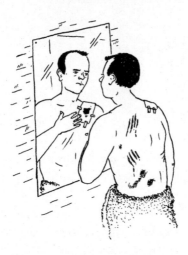

Did Something Attack You?

The only way one can become a werewolf, other than having been fathered by a male lycanthrope (see Chapter 4, "Purebloods"), is to have the blood or saliva of a fully transformed, wild werewolf enter your bloodstream, in most cases through a bite. If a wolf-like creature did not attack you in the past thirty days, chances are very good that you are not a lycanthrope. But if a ferocious, hairy animal attacked you, even if you were told that it was simply a dog, a bear, a wolf, or a coyote, read on. You need to be absolutely sure.

When Did the Attack Occur?

Lycanthropic transformation only occurs on the night of the full moon, as well as the nights before and after (the waxing and waning). If you were attacked on a non-transformation date or during daylight hours, then what you encountered was not a werewolf and you do not have lycanthropy. (For detailed information on full moons and transformation dates, refer to Chapter 6, "When It Will Happen and What It Will Feel

Like," or if the attack happened before 2011, the back appendix.) If an animal of some kind bit you during a known transformation date, it's possible that you were bitten by a werewolf. Keep reading.

--- **TRUE LEGENDS?** ---

THE LYCANTHROPE DWARF

We would love to be able to say that all werewolves grow to a certain height and weight, that if you were attacked and bitten by something shorter than six feet tall, it wasn't a werewolf and you're in the clear. Unfortunately, the legend of Harold Greenfield makes that impossible to say with certainty. In the early twentieth century, Harold Greenfield was born with achondrophasia, a bone-growth disorder. While still in his teens, the 3'9" tall Greenfield was attacked by a werewolf outside his rural Kansas home and contracted lycanthropy. After displaying rapid healing and enhanced senses, he was cast out by his terrified family. They believed these traits, along with his short stature, indicated that he was cursed by the devil. Tragically, at least for the first several years of his lycanthropy, Harold appeared to have believed them. When he changed into a werewolf for the first time, he grew no taller than a height of approximately 5'6" while standing on his back paws, making Greenfield one of the smallest werewolves ever known. But what he lacked in height, he made up for in ferocity. He tore his way across the American Southwest like a feral tornado, leaving behind a trail of sketchy newspaper reports that told stories of men, women, livestock, and horses who were "mangled," "ripped to pieces," and "slaughtered in the most grisly way imaginable." While some reports were plausible, citing coyotes as the attackers, others were outlandish, describing the aggressor as a "badger," "a giant beaver," and in one exceptional case, "a mammoth prairie rat." Interestingly, the attacks stopped after several years. Many lycanthropes who claimed to have met Harold in his dormant state reported later in life that he had not only learned to restrain himself during his Moon Sets, but had grown to almost six feet tall. Speculation abounded that his monthly transformations had, over time, grown and regrown his bones enough times that he eventually healed fully from his disorder.

After the Attack, Were There Any Reports of Naked Human Corpses in the Area?

When a werewolf is killed in his wild state, he changes back to his dormant form and, if discovered, is found in the nude, since his clothing is usually torn off during his transformation. (See Chapter 3, "The Stages of Lycanthropy.") In many cases, the only reason a victim survives the ordeal of a werewolf attack in the first place is that the beast was killed before finishing the job, leaving behind a nude corpse. If a nude corpse was found at the site of your attack, it is almost certain that you were attacked by a werewolf, and you will experience your first transformation within a month.

If no nude corpses were found, it is possible that the werewolf who attacked you is still alive. If this is the case, he may attempt to contact you, to offer guidance in the ways of lycanthropy. It might be the case that the only reason you're reading this book is that the lycanthrope who attacked you later tracked you down and slipped it into your mailbox. Despite how you might be feeling about your attacker right now, by giving you this book, he has done you a huge favor. (For more on this, see Chapter 17, "So You've Attacked Someone.")

THAT'S PROBABLY THE SPECIAL VICTIMS UNIT KNOCKING ON YOUR DOOR

If you do wake up next to a naked corpse, you're going to be getting a lot of attention from the police and possibly the media, since you're now the prime suspect in what they perceive to be a fantastic sex crime. On the bright side, you won't have to worry about anyone suspecting you're a werewolf, since the intense interest generated by sexual murders often distracts from any suspicion of a werewolf's involvement. People see what they want to see. Use this to protect yourself. Just be prepared to suffer through some very uncomfortable questions about your background and your "proclivities."

Hospital Time: How Quickly Did You Heal?

One of the primary symptoms of lycanthropy, and one of the first you will develop, is an accelerated immune system combined with extremely rapid healing. If doctors tell you they are amazed at the speed of your recovery or that they have "never seen anything like this," that should be a red flag. If you were bitten by a werewolf, your wounds will probably have healed within twenty-four hours, and in just a few days there will be no evidence you were ever assaulted. On its own, quick healing might not be evidence of lycanthropy, but combined with other indicators, it must not be ignored.

Your Dreams: What Are They About?

Many Stage 1 lycanthropes report having exceptionally vivid dreams and nightmares, often of an animalistic, violent, and sexual nature. You may experience dreams of hunting, hearing wolves or other savage animals speaking as though they were people, and seeing fleeting images of yourself running close to the ground at a speed far faster than you ever

THE HEALING TEST!

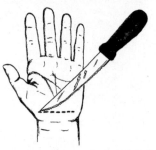

All lycanthropes are tremendously fast healers. Take a sharp knife and give your nondominant hand a shallow cut, just deep enough to draw blood along the base of your palm, parallel to (but not directly on) your wrist. Bandage and apply pressure. Before you were bitten, a cut like this used to take weeks to completely heal, but now you will find the wound sealed within twenty-four hours, and you'll be picking off the scab within three days tops. Put simply, your ability to naturally heal is speeding up, along with your metabolism. While this is simply a test, it is important to remember this if you wake up after a Moon with a serious wound. If it didn't kill you already, you're going to be in good shape. Remember this test, apply herbal or over-the-counter medical treatments, and *do not go to a hospital.*

propelled yourself in waking life. (For a fuller description of the dreams that lycanthropes experience and how to deal with their effects, see Chapter 7, "Werewolf Dreams and Stranger Things.") As dreams are often forgotten not long after waking, we cautiously recommend keeping a dream journal, so long as proper precautions are taken to keep it private.

Initial Sensory Enhancement

A heightened sense of smell will be the first thing you will notice as your condition advances toward your first transformation, and it will continue to evolve and surprise you as you enter the later stages. You will also notice a "layering" of the scents you experience, something that can be overwhelming in a hospital. As you lie there in your bed, wounded from the attack, you have nothing else to do but experience all the different smells, from wounds to medicine and chemicals to hospital food to the smell of sterile cleanliness. In fact, by using your nose, you may even be able to determine which spots around the hospital room were missed by the swipe of the mop or the squirt of industrial cleaning liquid.

> **HOSPITAL SAFETY TIP: DON'T ASK THE DOCTOR!** If you end up in a hospital and you smell something extraordinary, or manage to detect something with your nose that you would never have noticed in the past, it's OK to ask someone else if they notice it. But just to be safe, don't ask a doctor or nurse, stick to visitors or your fellow patients. Remember, the less that the doctors know about your lycanthropy, the better.

As you learn to use your nose, you will find that things you previously thought smelled heavenly and odors you found foul will become fascinating, as your nose will be able to unravel each element of a smell into its component parts.

A dramatically enhanced sensory experience is a very clear symptom of lycanthropy.

Do You See Dead People?

While odd dreams, nightmares, and quick healing can be easy to ignore, being visited by the chatty spirit of a dead acquaintance is pretty tough to get around. Many newly bitten lycanthropes claim to have both seen and/or conversed with ghosts, usually those who were recent victims of a werewolf attack. They arrive looking much the same way as after they were attacked (generally mangled and shredded) and often speak to you about your condition. In some cases, they urge you to kill yourself. Although this is very alarming, at this writing we have not been able to categorically prove that these experiences are anything more than intense hallucinations or exceptionally vivid dreams brought on by the onset of lycanthropy. Also, we have never had a report of a lycanthrope being physically harmed by a ghost. They can't hurt you.

Still, if you have been visited by a phantom who claims you are now a werewolf, and if an animal has attacked you on a confirmed transformation date, you can pretty much stop wondering. You are going to become a werewolf on the night before the next full moon, and you need to start preparing for that. (For more on encounters with the undead, refer to Chapter 7, "Werewolf Dreams and Stranger Things," and Chapter 20, "The Trouble with Vampires.")

Animalization

As you progress through the first several weeks toward your first transformation, you will probably experience several of the following traits, known as "animalization," or as some lycs call them, "wolf-outs." These are nothing to be afraid of, and you will learn to mask or control them as your body adjusts to its new abilities and urges.

Sharp bursts of rage accompanied by vocal tics. While erratic mood swings and extreme anger are common symptoms of any survivor of trauma, these flare-ups are more extreme with Stage 1 lycanthropes and are often accompanied by guttural vocal tics from the back of the throat, which can resemble tight, controlled growls or barks. Calm down. You are not a dog, and you're not going to be chasing cars or biting the mailman anytime soon. It's just an adjustment to your new condition, and you will learn to control it.

Accelerated hair and fingernail growth. This is just what it sounds like. If you still need confirmation that you are a lycanthrope, trim your fingernails right now. If you are ready to cut them again in two days, you are exhibiting one of the prime side effects of Stage 1 lycanthropy. Additionally, if a bald spot starts growing back, or you have additional beard growth or body hair appearing, that should be a red flag.

Marking your territory. There is no better way to put this than to just say it. If you are a lycanthrope, you are going to start to feel the urge to urinate on things. This behavior manifests itself more frequently with males than females, but the urge will be there, regardless of gender, usually as soon as the second week. Depending upon where you live, it is safe to say that society is generally hostile to this behavior. You are spreading your scent and marking your territory the way an animal would, and you will find that having your own scent surrounding you enables you to relax. This behavior can potentially jeopardize your quality of life. Luckily, since you also have a tremendously heightened sense of smell, you will learn that it really doesn't take much urine to get the job done. If you apply it properly, your co-workers will never notice a thing. (For more information on how to curb and control this urge, see Chapter 18, "Avoiding Detection.")

> **Famous Lycs Through Time**
> Allen Ginsberg, Poet
> (1926–97, Lyc years: 1944–97)
> Always thought people were reading too much into "Howl."

Reaction of pets and animals. Most animals simply do not like lycanthropes, particularly other mammals. Housecats will hiss and/or hide from you, dogs will occasionally bark in an aggressive manner, but in most cases will cower and whine, and horses will absolutely freak out. Luckily, as you progress through the stages of lycanthropy, this phenomenon can fade in both horses and dogs. Cats, unfortunately, will hate you forever. Tell people you're allergic.

Why Me?

By now, you should be well aware of the reality of your condition. Congratulations on getting through the denial phase. But an important part of accepting that you are now a werewolf is to avoid excessive self-pity.

In the early stages of lycanthropy, it's hard not to get lost in the apparent injustice that you, of all people, should be forced to deal with the inconvenience of such a complicated condition. *"But I have a spouse. A family. People are counting on me."* The sad fact of lycanthropy is it can come crashing into your life any time you happen to be unlucky enough to cross the path of a werewolf in his wild state. The werewolf doesn't care how much you love your wife and children or all the people who might be counting on you. In the wild werewolf's eyes, all humans and animals are just meat for feeding. The family man tastes just as good as the vagrant. People with sick mothers who need care, teachers of inner-city kids who are being inspired to learn for the first time, women who are carrying the children of soldiers since killed in combat overseas—any one of them can become the next lycanthrope if they just happen to take the wrong route home when the moon is looking full.

The thing to remember is that lycanthropy is a manageable condition to which you can and will adapt. It doesn't erase or replace the life you've been living and the happiness you've enjoyed. It's simply a new path for you and your loved ones to walk together.

CHAPTER THREE

The Stages of Lycanthropy

My secret? I've had a glass of bourbon and a cigar every night after dinner for the last 130 years. Also, I never settle in for a Moon without a fifty-pound tray of brisket from Lonnie's Smoke House Barbecue by my side. That brisket, along with a few bags of kibble, has saved many lives by keeping my stomach good and full.

—Cooper D., Retired Podiatrist

Age: 156, Lyc age: 138

LIFE EXPECTANCY AND LONGEVITY

Lycanthropes measure aging in two ways: their human age, measuring the time since they were born, and their lyc age, measuring the time since they were bitten. So a lycanthrope can be sixty years old with a lyc age of three years if they weren't bitten until they were fifty-seven. Obviously, for purebloods the human age and lyc age are the same.

If there's one thing you can brag about as a werewolf, it's your longevity. Lycanthropes can live far longer than humans can, assuming they keep from getting killed (not an easy task). Longevity is not the same as life expectancy. The average life expectancy of a werewolf is somewhere around forty days, owing to the fact that so many lycanthropes die during their first trio of Moons, with many of the rest of them getting killed before or during their second. But a werewolf who manages not to get himself killed can live for 150 years or more before succumbing naturally. This is the result of the astounding healing capability of lycanthrope biology.

Settle in. It's gonna be a long ride.

The process of changing back and forth is like the human body's healing process put on fast-forward. Cells and tissue are broken down and rebuilt, sealing up wounds and fighting any nascent diseases before they are allowed to spread or cause damage. In short, being a lycanthrope makes you heal faster, helping you to live longer, if you stay out of danger. Hopefully, as this book finds its way into the paws of more and more werewolves, the life expectancy of lycanthropes will begin to catch up with their longevity. (For more details on lycanthrope healing, see Chapter 16, "Health, Medicine, and Wellness.")

The Stages of Werewolf Life

There is a very big learning curve for the newly bitten werewolf. As you hastily learn to adapt to your new situation, your life expectancy increases the longer you manage to stay alive.

The lifespan of a lycanthrope can be broken down into five stages:

Stage 1: The First Thirty Days

If you're a freshly bitten lycanthrope, the first month is the most dangerous time in your life. You have only thirty days

Stage 1—Thirty days to get ready

from getting bitten to accept, and prepare for, the fact that you are about to transform into a bloodthirsty beast. Denial is one of the biggest killers of Stage 1 lycanthropes, second only to shotguns.

Lycanthropes often get loose on their first Moon, and many of them end up getting shot. If you meet a very old lycanthrope and ask him how he made it through his first Moon, he'll probably answer with one word: luck.

Stage 2: One to Eight Moon Sets
If you've made it past Stage 1, way to go! By now you (hopefully) know what you are and what you're capable of, and you're probably scared to death. Perfect! Fear is the best incentive to sweep everything else off the table and devote a single-minded focus to figuring out exactly what you have to do to stay alive.

The most dangerous part of your life is over. Now comes the really annoying part. This is a time of trial and error, of designing restraint systems, building cages, and trying to change your work schedule so that you can have three nights in a row off every month. It's also a turbulent time emotionally. In Stage 2 you must make some big decisions about whether

your career, place of residence, and even your personal relationships are right for your new lifestyle. There are many ways
for a Stage 2 lycanthrope to slip up, but just by getting past
Stage 1, your life expectancy has increased exponentially.

During this stage you'll still have no memory of what occurs during your Moons and no control over your actions in
your wild state. That will begin to change in the next stage.

Stage 3: Becoming a Smarter Werewolf
(More Than Eight Moon Sets)

The Stage 3 or "mature" lycanthrope is one who has managed to survive more than eight Moon Sets. If you've made it
to Stage 3, you've probably established a manageable routine
and designed a sustainable restraint system to keep from getting loose, discovered, or killed. You now have great potential
to live a long, peaceful life. You might even be lucky enough
to die in your bed of natural causes more than a hundred years
from now.

Stage 3 can last for several decades, and as you age more
and more Moons, the line between your dormant and wild
states begins to blur. After several years as a werewolf, you'll
begin to remember more of what happens during your
Moons. When in your wild state, you'll have more capacity
for rational thought, care, and cunning. This isn't to say that
you'll ever possess the same intelligence in your wild state as
in your dormant state, but you will be a little smarter and
more aware of the dangers posed by the world around you.

What's happening is, after years of Moons, you're more
willing to accept both sides of yourself as the same being.
During your early Moons in Stage 1 and Stage 2, you are so
stunned by what you're turning into that your mind goes into
a kind of shock, surrendering all control to your wild urges to
hunt and kill. Your dormant consciousness believes you've
crossed a line into a completely new existence and simply

shuts down, which is why you don't remember anything and have no remnant of your higher intelligence in these early Moons. You're basically just a really strong, hungry dog.

When the shock wears off and you get used to the process, you're able to hang on to more of your dormant consciousness in your wild state. This allows you to keep memories from your wild state, and you begin to learn from your previous Moons, applying knowledge gained in your wild state. You also hang on to more of your higher faculties, which means you might eventually learn to use your opposable thumbs to some degree and perhaps even free yourself from your restraints. Sounds dangerous, but not to worry. Though you might be able to get free, you'll also be more aware of what awaits you if you do.

You'll never be completely in control of yourself when wild. But the longer you live, the more control you'll have.

Stage 4: Middle Age, Midlife Crisis, and Lycanthrope Ascendance

This stage is hard to pin down on a time line, as it hits different people at different points in life and some might never experience it. The Stage 4 lycanthrope has been living with lycanthropy for several decades. By Stage 4, your monthly routine has become as natural as waking up in the morning. It's just life. You can barely remember when you didn't have to lock yourself away thrice a month. You're a more intelligent werewolf, more in control when wild, and you learn something new from every Moon. You're doing fine. Except you are reaching a kind of crossroads.

Stage 4 is basically the midlife crisis of lycanthropy. When you reach a lyc age of around forty years, you might start to feel like you're looking back and forward at the same time. You start getting wistful, remembering the life you used to dream you'd have and comparing that to the way things are.

You begin to overestimate the control you have in your wild state, and you start to think it might be nice to shake things up a bit.

That's what makes this stage very dangerous. The last thing a lycanthrope needs is a shake-up to his routine.

You might begin to resent that you have to lock yourself away every month. In the face of your own mortality, you might also resent that you'll go to your grave without anyone ever knowing your true nature, in all its strength and vitality. This goes far beyond the common human response to a midlife crisis (getting a sports car, a divorce, hair plugs). As a Stage 4 lycanthrope, you might begin to take your own security for granted, perhaps even allowing yourself to run loose from time to time just to see what'll happen. In short, you might want to see what it's like to let the wolf out.

It is at this point in life that some werewolves begin to seriously consider "Lycanthrope Ascendance." Many werewolves come to a point where they decide it is wrong to hide who they are. They feel that they are a product of nature, that their race has survived evolutionary "weeding out" processes, and therefore they have just as much a right to exist on this earth as do non-lycs. They might even have feelings of superiority over the rest of humanity, seeing as they are the predators and non-lycs are the prey. The common argument is, nowhere else in nature does the predator take measures to protect the prey from itself, and therefore non-lyc humans should be beholden to protect themselves from werewolves, not the other way around.

Lycanthrope Ascendance is discussed more in-depth in Chapter 23, but suffice it to say that this philosophy is a foolish and dangerous line of thought, jeopardizing the safety and the humanity of lycanthropes. It's true—a tiger doesn't go out of its way to battle its own nature in order to protect the gazelle. But if the gazelle knew how to fire a shotgun, and if the tiger became nearly as vulnerable as the gazelle twenty-seven days out of the month, the tiger might reconsider.

Stage 4 is part of the maturity process. It's the gateway to your golden years. After passing through this stage successfully, you'll be rewarded with many decades of peace and calm.

Stage 5: Lyc Age of More Than Fifty Years
(The Elders of Lycanthropy)

The very fact that a lycanthrope has survived into his golden years indicates that he possesses an exceptional temperament and an ingenuity that few can match. True acceptance comes at this point in a lycanthrope's life.

When you have lived well beyond the human age of one hundred, you might find that you can undergo your Moons without restraints. The combination of increased intelligence and decreased metabolism will make you a much more docile werewolf. Your metabolism has slowed with age, and the urge to go out and hunt is far weaker. There have even been some older werewolves who claim their Moons no longer occur.

Stage 5—Taking it slow

They still feel a change around a full moon, but they don't transform anymore so much as they "hibernate," sleeping straight through the night of their Moons with no evidence of having stirred.

The elder lycanthrope deserves respect. His very existence is proof that you could have a long, full life ahead of you if you take care of yourself. Your life doesn't end when you get bitten. It's just the beginning.

Dying with Lycanthropy: What Happens When a Werewolf Is Killed?

We're not going to get into metaphysics and try to discuss where you go when you die, except to say "the ground." But we will address the death of a werewolf.

The stories are true. When you die during your Moon, you transform back into your dormant physical state, though usually not all the way to your pristine, middle-of-the-month state.

When a werewolf dies in his wild state, his body goes into a sort of panic mode. It knows that it is in severe physical danger and reacts by transforming back into the dormant state. It's an involuntary attempt to break down and rebuild the body in the hope of reversing the damage. It's akin to the way the human body will go into shock or enjoy a surge of adrenaline to endure extreme pain.

A dead lycanthrope is found in his human form, but usually with slightly elongated limbs and a stretched jaw. He is recognizable, but just slightly different-looking. The changed appearance is usually explained away by pathologists as a corpse's shocking pallor and natural bloating. Your fur will also have fallen off and turned to stiff, thin twigs all around you. Only someone who is suspicious would identify those twigs as dried hair strands on sight.

If you die in your dormant state, outside of your Moon, you do not suddenly transform to your wild state. Should you die when dormant, there will be no observable difference between your corpse and the corpse of a non-lyc (absent an autopsy review of your biochemistry). Chances are, the lycanthrope who has managed to keep his secret all his life will not betray that secret when he finally goes to the grave.

CHAPTER FOUR

Purebloods

The Life and Trials of the Baby Werewolf

My dad taught me early on what I'd be in for when I became a man. We started setting up my safe room when I was seven, in the basement of my grandma's house. It used to be his safe room when he was seventeen. It didn't need a lot of work, but he wanted me to get used to the kind of upkeep I'd have to devote to it in order to keep safe on my Moons. He taught me one of the things that keeps a werewolf safe is the pride he takes in his own precautions. So we pretty much took it apart and rebuilt it from scratch. He had me start strapping in there for a year and a half before my first Moon. I couldn't wait. Every month I hoped that this would be the one, but it seemed to never come. I worried that something was wrong with me. My dad even seemed to grow impatient. Looking back, I wonder if my dad started to suspect I wasn't his, like maybe my mom had an affair with a non-lyc milkman or something. If so, that suspicion got squashed like a grape. Two months after my fourteenth birthday, I had my first change, and I was glad to be so well prepared.

—Colin I., Environmental Lawyer
Age: 37, Lyc age: 37

WHAT IS A PUREBLOOD?

A pureblood is a lycanthrope who was born with the condition. The pureblood does not experience his first Moon until puberty.

Even though he is called a pureblood, both of his parents cannot be lycanthropes. The pureblood is almost always born of a lycanthrope father and a non-lycanthrope mother. The female lycanthrope cannot carry a child, simply because a fetus cannot survive the mother's twenty-seven transformations during pregnancy. Rarely does it survive even one transformation. The only way for a baby to be conceived from two lyc parents is if the father and mother use in vitro fertilization to fertilize her egg with the father's sperm, and the fertilized egg is then implanted into the uterus of a non-lycanthrope surrogate mother.

What to Expect If You're a Pureblood

Your first change won't occur until you reach puberty. That can be as young as age ten, or as old as age sixteen or seventeen. Until the time of your first Moon, you won't be very outwardly different from other kids your age, except that your abnormally strong physique and enhanced sensory perception will probably make you one of the better athletes in your school.

As you approach puberty, your body might appear even more awkward and gawky than your average pubescent, since your physical development will be a little more drastic than

---

DON'T BELIEVE IT!

A lycanthrope baby born on a Moon will not be born in its werewolf state, and the OB-GYN will not find himself holding a growling, writhing baby wolf-child. Mothers of lyc babies shudder to imagine the damage that could be done by the child's claws and fangs during delivery. DON'T BELIEVE IT! Pureblood lycanthropes do not experience their first werewolf transformation until puberty. Your lycanthrope child will look no less human than every other baby in the maternity ward.

The pubescent lycanthrope in his natural environment

most. It will pay off in the long run, since by the time you've reached adolescence you'll have the strength, musculature, and endurance of an Olympic athlete. (Note: to avoid drawing suspicion, it's best not to excel *too* much athletically. Nothing wrong with being the starting quarterback or the top-scoring forward on your basketball team, just don't break too many division records.)

Your prepubescent years should be spent learning about lycanthropy and preparing for your first change. You need to realize the enormity of a lycanthrope's responsibility to himself and his loved ones and neighbors. Hopefully, your father or a lycanthrope guardian will be there to guide you in these years.

Why Puberty?

There is a direct relationship between a pubescent child's hormonal changes and the onset of his monthly transformations.

At the age when the typical pubescent child's pituitary gland releases gonadotropins (luteinizing hormones, or "LH," and follicle-stimulating hormones, or "FSH") into the blood-stream, the pureblood's pituitary gland releases an additional hormone, lycantropin. While the gonadotropins trigger the testes and ovaries to begin production of testosterone and estrogen, lycantropin acts upon the thyroid gland to begin a cyclical glandular process in the pureblood's body, which sets into motion his or her monthly transformation cycle. It would appear that the wait until puberty is an evolutionary mechanism, preventing pureblood lycanthropes from having their first Moon before the body is developed enough to survive the transformation. Just as a young girl experiences a widening of the hips as she enters her childbearing years, developing the frame necessary to carry a child to term, prepubescent lycanthropes have to develop the bone and tissue structure that can endure the violent breakdown and rebuilding of these structures during a Moon.

Parenting Tips

Helping Your Pureblood Live Responsibly and Without Fear

You need to begin teaching your pureblood child from a young age (seven or eight years old) about who he is and what lies ahead. This may sound daunting and perhaps even a little cruel, but the far crueler option would be to let your child grow up unprepared for his Moons.

It is much more difficult to convince an adult who has been bitten that he is now a lycanthrope than it is to convince a child that he's one day going to start turning into a wild werewolf. A young child has the imagination and credulity to believe what his father tells him, even if it is something as seemingly outlandish as this. The older the child gets, the less likely he is to believe it—and the more tragic it will seem. A child nearing puberty is already confused and dismayed by the changes to his body. That's not the time to spring on him the news of his coming monthly transformations. Much better to have the conversation early.

Famous Lycs Through Time

Louisa May Alcott, Novelist

(Pureblood: 1832–88)

Once woke up in a puddle of limbs behind the dormitory of a finishing school. Soon after was inspired to begin her first draft of *Little Women*.

The young child can approach his coming Moons with anticipation, and he can see his preparation for the change like a project, especially if you're there to lead him through it. Working with your child to build his safe room, teaching him about his restraints, and most of all, showing by example the precautions you take will inculcate your child with the reality of lycanthropy: It is a natural, manageable condition that comes with a great deal of responsibility, and it is your child's duty as a lycanthrope to accept this responsibility.

How Are Purebloods Different from the Bitten?

The most striking difference between purebloods and the bitten concerns the transformation process. The bitten will usually describe his transformation as being far more painful and nightmarish than will the pureblood. It seems that the pureblood has a smoother transformation because lycanthropy has been a part of his body since birth, whereas the bitten had lycanthropy introduced to his body over the course of a brief, thirty-day process that is akin to the spread of a virus.

Some less striking differences include:

• More even distribution of body hair on purebloods than the patchy growth on a bitten lyc.
• Stronger sense of pride/sense of self among the purebloods.

- The bitten are far more prone to suffer depression.
- Since they haven't had the guidance that purebloods have, the bitten are usually more open to experimenting with their Moon procedures. They'll try out new restraint systems to increase their comfort. They'll switch up food options to maximize their budget. This experimentation has led to many beneficial developments in lycanthrope accessories and cuisine.
- The bitten are far more likely to die during their first Moons.

If you ask a pureblood, however, he would probably say there is no difference, since the pureblood is often raised by a bitten lyc, usually the man that the pureblood has emulated throughout his life.

———— TRUE LEGENDS? ————

THE LIL' WEREPUP ORPHANAGE
AND PRIMARY SCHOOL

There is believed to be a secret lycanthrope-run orphanage for purebloods, called the Li'l Werepup Orphanage and Primary School. Its location is unknown. Some say it is housed on a compound owned by a wealthy industrial scion (it was once rumored to be run by John E. du Pont, the eccentric member of the prominent du Pont family, but after he was sent to prison for murder in 1997, his grounds were fully explored and documented, and that rumor was dispelled). Others believe the orphanage to be a mobile operation, never staying in one place, to avoid hunters.

Wherever it may be, the Werepup Orphanage takes pureblood lycanthropes off the hands of lyc parents who don't want the responsibility of raising their children properly. Since it requires absolute secrecy to survive, the organization acquires a new pureblood child via kidnapping. The lyc father or the baby's mother will send word to the organization via a one-sided communication (see below), then they wait. After several months, without warning, soldiers of the orphanage will break into the home of the parents and kidnap the child.

The child is then taken under the care and tutelage of the orphanage, where he is taught everything he needs to know to live safely and responsibly as a lycanthrope. He is taught how to fashion his own restraints and build his own safe room. And, of course, he is given the proper schooling necessary to fulfill standard education requirements. When old enough, the orphanage helps the child find a home and occupation appropriate for the lycanthrope lifestyle.

It is unclear whether the orphanage is run entirely by lycanthropes. One would imagine not, since at least some humans would need to stand guard during the Moons.

If you're the parent of a pureblood lycanthrope and you are considering abandoning the child, the Li'l Werepup Orphanage might be able to help you. The only known way to get a message to them is to place a personals advertisement with the newspaper in your region that has the largest circulation. The heading of the personals ad must read *a real montgomery, ready to heed his guinevere*. There should be no other text in the ad, and you should publish no contact information to avoid being tracked by werewolf hunters. If you use your region's largest newspaper, the orphanage will know how to obtain your contact information through their own contacts within the newspaper's offices. Once they do, they will find you and take your child off your hands, if they see fit to do so.

CHAPTER FIVE

Tips on Your First Transformation

The first time I changed, it was prom night. 1986. Jenny Milbank. I can still smell everything. Her hair spray—her hair was all up, in that crazy '80s way, you know? And she had this perfume on that just filled the air. I was antsy all day, figured it was nerves. We took pictures on her parents' front lawn before the limo picked us up. She had this blue dress that matched my tie. It was her idea to do that. The moon came up on the drive to the dance. Middle of the highway, going seventy-five mph.

The funny thing is, when they did an autopsy on the driver, it turned out he'd been drinking. Open and shut case. Her parents got a bunch of money from the limo company, and while I guess I feel bad about that, I'm glad they got something. They lost their only daughter, for Christ's sake. And the guy was drinking, right? I can still hear her voice from back in that car. She turns to me with that big, beautiful smile and says it:

"Hey, check it out—a moon roof."

—Jeffrey K., Real Estate Broker
Age: 38, Lyc age: 22

LAST-MINUTE PREPARATIONS

If you have flipped to this page because the full moon is approaching, you suspect you are about to turn into a werewolf, and haven't had time to properly prepare your surroundings, read on. Please note, though, that this chapter offers quick fixes only, techniques that will attempt to keep you, your

---

EMERGENCY SHOPPING LIST

- Moving truck
- Extra cash (at least $200)
- Combination padlock
- Cell phone
- Raw meat (as much as you can get your hands on)

---

loved ones, and any potential innocent victims alive, *in that order.*

Throughout the course of your new life, you will need to create more elaborate techniques, preparations, and schedules in order to manage your Moons with maximum safety and efficiency, and to enable you to get as much as possible from the rest of your life, the majority of which will be spent in dormant form. Down the line, you may need to radically alter your home, job, relationships, and philosophies to accommodate your condition, and this guide will help you with that. There will be much work to be done. But for now, you're turning into a wild, ravenous beast, possibly in as little as a few hours, and this is what you need to do to stay alive.

This first change and the period leading up to it will certainly be the hardest part of your ordeal. If you survive these first few trying nights, your odds of survival increase more than tenfold. Thousands before you have survived this experience. You can too.

WHEN IT WILL HAPPEN

You will transform into a werewolf on the evening before the full moon, the evening of the full moon, and the evening after the full moon. These three transformations will happen roughly thirty days after you were initially attacked. The transformation will begin anywhere from forty minutes to two hours after the sun sets. Be ready early. Eventually, you will be able to sense the change coming and perhaps even regulate its onset, but for at least the first several months, it will be out of your control.

GET AWAY FROM OTHER PEOPLE

Your first transformation is not something to be shared with others, particularly your friends or loved ones. Down the line, it will be important to make decisions about who you want to tell about your condition, if anyone, but the first time is not the right time.

FIND A SAFE, ENCLOSED SPACE IN A REMOTE AREA

If you do not have access to an enclosed safe room, heavy cage, or similar structure as detailed in Chapter 9, "A Safe Room of One's Own," the best way to deal with your first

---

IT'S NO ONE'S JOB BUT YOURS

Countless lycanthropes have been killed upon their first or second transformations after giving a loved one a gun and instructing them to "use it on me if you have to." This is a terrible strategy. It creates a situation in which you will be shot to death, and the person you love will be wanted for your murder. Keep in mind that after you die, you will shortly revert to your dormant (non-wolf) form, leaving your companion holding a smoking gun in front of your naked corpse, while the neighbors summon the police. That's no way to treat a friend.

transformation is to rent a medium-size moving truck, drive it to a remote location well before sunset, and lock yourself in the back. When picking out a truck, avoid selecting one with windows in the back, as you will certainly shatter them.

We do not recommend stealing the truck, because if you are caught, you will either transform and be killed in a prison lockup or worse, transform and *survive* in a prison lockup, only to find yourself the subject of military, government, or medical experiments. Avoid drawing the attention of the police at all costs by adhering to the laws in your state as much as possible.

After you change, you will attempt to batter your way out of your truck, which will make a considerable amount of noise, so a remote location is very, very important. If you live in a city or densely populated area, get as far from people as possible and look for locations that are abandoned in the evenings. The parking lots of public golf courses and water parks are ideal, as there is plenty of space, parking, and there are no people around at night. Look for places that are seasonally abandoned as well. If it is wintertime and you live on a coast, go park by the beach. If it is possible to move off the road slightly and camouflage your truck, all the better.

Additionally, make sure you have the ability to lock the truck from the inside and to open the truck once you've changed back to your dormant state. Most moving trucks have a release lever on the inside, which we recommend locking with a combination padlock. In your wild state you will not have the mental capacity to even grasp the concept of a combination padlock, much less be able to remember how to open one, and you also will not have to worry about hanging on to a key. While it is unlikely that you will be able to figure out any kind of latch system in your wild state, it is not impossible (werewolves do have opposable thumbs), and the extra insurance that a padlock brings could mean the difference between life and death.

BRING A CELL PHONE AND SOME CASH

With any luck, on the morning after your Moon you won't have to do anything but climb into the front of your truck and head home. But any number of things can go wrong, so as a precaution, bring your cell phone, make sure you have service, and make sure it's charged. And bring extra cash (approximately $200). If the next morning arrives and you need to hail a cab, get some more raw meat, lay low in a hotel room, bribe a nosy reporter, or get out of town, cash is king. Stash both in the front of the truck, out of sight.

TAKE YOUR CLOTHES OFF, FOLD THEM NEATLY, AND STASH THEM OUT OF THE WAY

You must take your clothes off prior to transforming or you will tear through them. There is no point in destroying perfectly good clothes. Folding clothes and putting them away can be an important ritual, as it provides a reminder that no matter what you may be about to go through, you are not an animal—you are a civilized person. If you were planning on dying tonight, there would be no point in folding your clothes, but as you fully intend to go through your Moon safely, you need to make sure your clothes are neatly folded and waiting for you when you awake the next morning. We have been told by numerous lycanthropes that this simple ritual can make a world of difference. If you are using a moving truck, we recommend neatly placing your clothes under the front seat before locking yourself in the back.

WHAT SHOULD I WEAR?

It really doesn't matter. But for many lycanthropes, having their wardrobe organized can make them feel more prepared. If you feel that having a fixed outfit beforehand will help soothe you, a good general rule of thumb is to wear something similar to what you might wear when going through airport security: loose-fitting clothing that can be easily removed and folded, shoes or sandals without laces that can be slipped off, and nothing you would be too upset about ruining. It's also a good idea to stay away from any item of clothing that may be associated with you personally. No two werewolves are exactly the same, and in the unlikely event that you go through your change while still clothed, it's possible that all your clothes might not completely tear off your body. You may find yourself in some hot water if the savage werewolf seen menacing the town was spotted wearing your shredded CCHS CLASS OF '92 REUNION T-shirt.

TAKE OFF ALL JEWELRY, INCLUDING YOUR WEDDING RING

As you will be nearly doubling in size, you will likely outgrow any jewelry that you wear. If the jewelry is strong enough to endure your increased mass it could severely constrict blood flow. Rings are particularly dangerous, seeing as your fingers will not only be growing longer, but will be getting considerably thicker as well. If you're lucky, the ring will either be forced off or split as you change, but it will more likely become wedged into the flesh of your finger as your paw expands, resulting in painful constriction and numbness of the digit. There have been many cases of lycanthropes actually biting their own fingers off and in some cases swallowing them. While your accelerated healing ability will prevent you from bleeding to death, your fingers will not grow back, even

Remove all jewelry

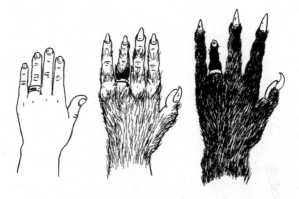

in your dormant form. Additionally, if you want your wedding ring back, the only way to find it will be by searching though your stool over the next several weeks, a process that is as unsanitary as it is unsettling.

BUY LOTS OF RAW, RED MEAT

The primary sensations you will experience in your wild state are hunger and rage. We heartily recommend having some form of livestock on hand to serve as immediate prey, but since getting your hands on a live farm animal can be tricky on short notice, hit the grocery store and buy lots of raw, red meat. Visit a Costco or another big-box store that sells in bulk for cheap. You will be far less dangerous if you have something to eat during your Moon. Cheap steak or ground beef will do the trick. You'll need at least fifty pounds to safely satisfy your hunger in your wild state. (See Chapter 11, "Diet and Livestock.")

It's also helpful to eat a big meal beforehand. If you are hungry while in dormant form, you will be famished during

SERIOUSLY, TAKE OFF THE WEDDING RING

While many lycanthropes know instinctively to remove all jewelry, we specify the wedding ring for a reason. Many scared people who are going through their transformations for the first time leave their wedding ring on, hoping against hope that the symbol of their undying love will somehow enable them to cling to a vestige of their humanity or remind them not to attack or kill their spouse. This is hogwash. First off, no matter what form you assume, your humanity is only as lost as you allow it to be, and second, while love is indeed a powerful thing, it cannot stop a lycanthropic transformation or control the unleashed animal instinct of a savage werewolf any more than it can halt the pull of gravity.

your Moon. The more meat you have in your system before your Moon, the less you will need to hunt for it during. You will never completely lose the hunger, but having a full stomach may satisfy some of the desperation that drives the werewolf to batter out of his cage. Every little bit helps.

IF YOU HAVE NO MONEY AND CAN'T GET A TRUCK, WHERE CAN YOU GO?

You should seek out a place that people do not frequent during the night: Head to a basement or attic and, if you have time, restrain yourself with something sturdy. (For proper techniques see Chapter 10, "Strapping In.")

We suggest public schools, churches, abandoned warehouses, offices, or small businesses that close at night. Basically, any place that closes before the sun goes down, locks its doors at night, and doesn't have a regular night watchman, burglar alarm, security cameras, or valuables of any interest to thieves. A place where your presence won't raise suspicions would be best, but this is a worst-case scenario, so do the best that you can. If there is somewhere remote and/or abandoned that local lore says is "haunted," that will be ideal. If people are already scared to go somewhere, they'll be quicker to run if they hear something go bump in the night.

If your only choices are buildings that are still active in the daytime, enter during office hours, find a public restroom that is close to the basement or attic, go into one of the stalls, lock it, and stand or sit on the toilet with your feet out of sight. Use all of your senses to listen for or smell passersby. If it appears that they are not going away, you need to. You do not want to be anywhere near human beings when you change.

After the establishment has closed, *quietly* make your way to the cellar, attic, or room in which you are least likely to be heard making a great deal of noise and strap yourself in as best you can. After your first transformation, if you survive, do everything you can to create a better situation for yourself

---

TRANQUILIZERS AND KNOCKOUT PILLS:
JUST THIS ONCE

We do not recommend tranquilizers as a regular method for enduring your Moons, but if you haven't had enough time to prepare for this first change, it might be necessary. However, taking tranquilizers before you transform will not work, as the effects will be burned off during your change. You need to grind the drugs into some raw ground meat that you will devour after you transform. Remember that it takes roughly three times the amount of tranquilizer to knock you out in your wild state as it would in your dormant state. This is dangerous, difficult to do correctly, and may be habit-forming in the long run. It is recommended only as a last-minute option.

next time. No lycanthrope can survive this way with any kind of regularity, and even if you do, the chances that you will kill or pass on the condition are far, far greater.

If it is impossible to restrain yourself indoors and you must go somewhere outside, we highly recommend going anywhere where there are more animals than people around, especially farms with livestock or zoos. When you are in your wild state, you won't care what you attack. If you get lucky, you might just take down a couple of cows from a local dairy farm or slaughter a giraffe in a zoo. If you attempt this successfully and kill an animal, never do it again in the same place. If you kill an animal that is someone's property, they will surely take precautions so it doesn't happen again, and you don't want to be around for that.

Do Not Videotape or Record Yourself Transforming

Werewolves are tremendously difficult to control. Cameras have been broken and cameramen have been killed or infected trying to document transformations. There are some exceptions to this (see Chapter 13, "Romance and the Modern Lycanthrope"), but as a general rule, it can be a severe psychological jolt to see yourself transforming before you have adjusted to what you have become. Additionally, if it gets out onto the Internet or falls into the wrong hands, the consequences can be devastating for both you and your loved ones.

CHAPTER SIX

When It Will Happen
and What It Will Feel Like

You know when you're a little kid and one of your teeth gets loose?
You spend the whole day pokin' it, and it hurts, but it's that sweet
kind of hurt that you just can't stop touching. So you're wiggling
the tooth and, all of a sudden, it's time. You just feel it. There's a
snap, you can taste the blood, feel that tooth moving more than it
was moving before, and your eyes and nose kind of choke up with
fluid. You know that sickening little clucking sound as it pops in
and out of your gum, then finally breaks free? OK—now imagine
that it's not just that one little tooth, it's every single bone in your
body. Just cracking, moving, popping, and coming unglued. It's
pretty goddamned intense. To tell you the truth, I've kind of grown
to like it.

It's like being reborn.

—Gary H., Bartender
Age: 53, Lyc age: 19

WHEN WILL IT HAPPEN?

On the night before the full moon, you will transform into
your wild state for the first time. While the exact timing of
the change is different for everybody, it will not happen until
after darkness falls, when the moon is high. It is believed that
the abnormally high level of iron in the lycanthrope's bloodstream is why you are so sensitive to the moon's rise and pull.
But some see the fact that the change occurs only after dark

As the full moon nears, your body experiences a surge of lycantropin, triggering the change

as evidence of a Darwinian form of self-preservation. Were-wolves transforming at night simply live longer than if they were to transform during the day. No matter the scientific reasons for it, the fact that the change doesn't happen until after sundown helps to keep you safe.

Your transformations are dependent on the cycles of the moon. While we strongly recommend further study, the essential information you need to know is this: a lycanthrope *only* transforms into his wild state three nights per month—on the night of the full moon and the nights immediately before and after. As such, determining exactly when the full moon will occur is crucial to your survival.

If you are reading this book before the year 2011, flip to the back of the book for a complete appendix of transformation dates. If you ever find yourself without this book handy, there are numerous other sources, but it's always a good idea to double- and triple-check your information. No one source should ever be enough for you. If a publication gets it wrong, they'll print a correction. If you get it wrong, you could slaughter a family of five.

Here are some reliable secondary sources:

Almanacs: Popular and highly regarded almanacs include the *Old Farmer's Almanac*, the *New York Times Almanac* (formally known as the *Universal Almanac*), the *Time Almanac with Information Please*, and the *World Almanac and Book of Facts*. Flip directly to the section called "moon and tides" or "astronomy." All are excellent resources.

Nautical, Military, or Sportsmen's Guides to Moon and Tide: People who make their living on the ocean rely on the information in these guides for their safety and livelihood. If they can trust them, so can you. We particularly recommend the *Eldridge Tide and Pilot Book.* Updated annually since 1875 and republished every November, this classic book has kept sailors and fishermen (and yes, lycanthropes) alive and in the know for over a century.

The Internet: The information superhighway is almost certainly going to have what you need. Sadly, it also offers a great deal of inaccurate, copied, or unchecked information. Make sure you double- and triple-check your information. Wikipedia won't cut it this time.

THE TRANSFORMATION

The transformation itself is gradual, with the early signs arriving roughly eight hours before sunset and the final event happening anywhere from forty minutes to two hours after the sun goes down. Here's what to expect:

Eight Hours Before Sunset

The morning of the day of your first Moon of the month will begin fairly normally. You will experience an unusual acceleration of fingernail, toenail, and hair growth over the entire body. This shouldn't be extreme or even noticeable to anyone but a vigilant observer.

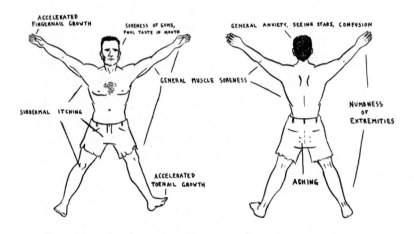

You will also begin to experience soreness, as your bones and muscles start to feel the pull of the transformation to come. The soreness will be felt all along your back and in your joints, particularly your knees, elbows, fingers, and toes. You will also begin to feel a dull ache at the base of the tailbone, or coccyx, as though you fell several feet to the floor and landed hard on your rear. This is due to the fact that in less than twelve hours, you will be growing a tail.

DRINKING AND HOWLING

It is important to remain hydrated on the day leading up to your change. Your transformation is very dehydrating, and the more hydrated you are beforehand, the less frantic you'll be for water after the change. For this reason, avoiding alcohol on the day of your Moon is also strongly recommended.

When in your wild state, having a water source, like a sturdy drinking trough or pile of crushed ice nearby, is very handy. In your wild state, you will only stop to drink after you've eaten a sufficient amount. Near the end of your Moon, you will drink, rest, collapse, and finally sleep. It is during this sleep that you will change back to dormant form, marking the end of the Moon.

Four Hours Before Sunset

The aching in the joints will begin to subside but may be replaced with a persistent, dull subdermal itching all over the body, particularly on the backs of the hands, fore-arms, armpits, pubic region, the backs of the knees, and from the back of the neck down the spine. You also may experience a slight extension of the teeth from the gums, and they may be sore to the touch. To relieve this, we recommend ice cream.

Two Hours Before Sunset

In the two hours leading up to the event, you should already be in the place where you plan to make your transformation. Try to remain comfortable and calm. Expect the following symptoms:

Evacuation. As your body prepares to change, it may begin to purge itself involuntarily, in the form of urination, vomiting,

or diarrhea. The involuntary nature of these purges will re-
cede with future transformations, but the first several times,
you should be ready for this. If you plan to lock yourself in an
area that does not come equipped with facilities, we recommend going to the bathroom early and often. Bring wet
towels.

Anxiety and Perspiration. Many Stage 1 lycanthropes report
a rising sense of fear, despite the lack of any immediate peril,
in some cases accompanied by numbness or perspiration. It is
important to realize that this is your body reacting to the
change, and not a reason to panic.

Confusion. The surge of lycantropin hormone will cause
heightened electrical activity in the brain, not unlike some of
the symptoms of epilepsy. While you will not experience a
seizure, you may have pre-seizure
symptoms, or "auras." This can be
anything from dizziness to seeing
stars to a foul or sour taste developing in your mouth just prior to transformation. More dangerous auras can
be extreme confusion or an inability
to focus on what is happening in the
present. You may experience difficulty determining if what you are experiencing is reality, a vivid memory
of a past event, or even a dream.
Whatever you do, *do not call an am-
bulance or go to an emergency room.*

Famous Lycs Through Time

Chester A. Arthur,
21st U.S. President
(1829–86, Lyc years: 1860–86)
Hosted the International
Meridian Conference in 1884,
where the Greenwich Meridian
was selected as the official
Prime Meridian, instituting
international standardized
time to allow lycs the world
over to plan their Moons more
accurately when traveling.

The Static. Immediately prior to the transformation, you will
begin to hear a persistent, slowly building hiss. It has been reported as sounding like "the ocean during a heavy squall," "an

army of snakes twisting across dry leaves," and one particularly morbid new lycanthrope described it as "standing at the base of a waterfall of blood." Whatever it sounds like to you, among the lycanthrope community, it is popularly known as "the Static."

As it starts, quietly at first, you will notice patches of hair developing all over your body, first in the areas where the worst of the itching occurred earlier and spreading from there. The static will grow in intensity and volume until it blocks out all other sounds with a wall of white noise. Some who heard it the first time reported it as feeling like they were drowning, despite being nowhere near the water, and one individual reported hearing "the agony of tortured souls, crying out from the pits of hell." Don't believe a word of it.

Source of "The Static"

The Static, despite any supernatural significance that some may attribute to it, is nothing more than the sound of rapid hair growth inside your ear canal. Given the other challenges you are about to face, it is nothing to be concerned about. If, right now, you were to lightly scratch your leg with your finger, it would make a tiny sound. Now give the same light scratch to the inside of your ear and listen to the difference. Now imagine that instead of your finger doing the scratching, dozens of coarse hairs were twisting and growing in there—and at the same time, your ability to hear was increasing to at least five times that of an average human being. While we're not qualified to say there is no such thing as a human soul crying out in pain as it is tortured for all eternity in hell, we can tell you for sure that the sound you're hearing isn't that.

Zero Hour: The Change As the Static increases, the transformation begins in earnest, and we're sorry to report that yes, it does hurt. There will be an intense bolt of pain that will strike you as your bones begin to snap and expand, something that generally forces the first-time lycanthrope down to all fours. Don't fight it. We recommend lying on the ground in a fetal position and rolling back and forth on your back.

Sudden pain, sweating   Sudden patches of hair growth

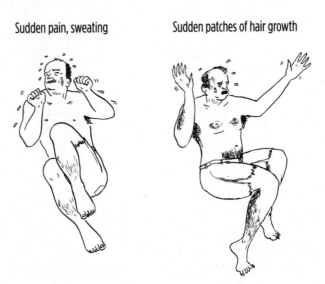

The more you attempt to resist the change, the more it will hurt. The bones in your back, shoulders, arms, legs, and face are breaking, stretching, rebuilding, and growing apart.

Your muscles are rebinding and expanding to fit your new, powerful skeleton. The lycantropin is now surging through your body, accompanied by a strong pulse of adrenaline, which serves to both soothe your pain and fuel the power as it courses through your veins.

Elongated limbs, revised physiognomy

Full coat of fur,
transformation complete

As the process completes itself, the pain and fear will fade, and you will fully succumb to your wild state. You will rise to your feet, commanded and compelled by the unbridled fury of nature itself. It's time to howl at the moon.

SO, WHAT WILL I LOOK LIKE?

Werewolves come in all shapes and sizes. The type of physicality you'll have after you transform is determined by a variety of factors. Depending on the genetic makeup of the werewolf that bit you, combined with the predeterminations mapped into your own DNA, the way you look in your wild state could be very different from what you might imagine. Some aspects of your dormant appearance will be reflected in your wild appearance. For example, an extremely bulky person will also be a rather imposing figure when wild, and a skinny lycanthrope will likely shape-shift into a rather slender werewolf. But other aspects of your appearance (snout size, fur patterns) are pretty much left to chance.

That said, there are four common werewolf body types out there. You are likely to fall into one of the following categories.

1. The Big Bad Wolf

This is the most common werewolf type. He has an elongated, wolf-like nose and lots of teeth. He's trim and prefers to sprint on his well-muscled hind legs before leaping into the air for a savage bite/slash attack with the front claws. Once knocking down his victim, the Big Bad Wolf often sinks his front claws deep into his victim's flesh and then shreds the stomach with his back claws. The coat is evenly tufted across the body.

2. The Pug

Despite the Pug's cute appearance, this is one of the most savage werewolf types in the lycanthrope kingdom. The shape of his nose resembles his nose while in dormant form much more than a wolf's traditional snout, and he has a flat little face. He looks like a man with a dog's face. The Pug is almost always bipedal, and a slower runner. Still, he makes up for his lack of speed with incredible endurance and tenacity. Like a bulldog, once he clamps his jaws down on something, he will not let it go. His preferred method of attack is to stalk prey, lie in wait, and either drop on top of his victims or unexpectedly leap from the shadows.

3. The Papa Bear

Possessing one of the most bone-chilling, gutteral howls in the lycanthrope kingdom, the Papa Bear is a formidable werewolf, and one of the most rare. An earthquake of bloody violence rumbling out of the brush, the Papa Bear is always a quadruped and probably couldn't stand up on his hind legs without the help of a crane. When he attacks, it's as graceful as a car crash. After building up speed, he launches his full weight at his prey, biting down at its shoulder, using his front claws to guide it under him, and coming down on it with the full force of his weight, crushing its rib cage, neck, or spine. As the prey lies helpless and shattered, the Papa Bear slowly gets back on all fours to feed.

4. The Lionthrope

The Lionthrope appears more glamorous than the rest of the lycanthrope kingdom, and he can even appear slightly cat-like in appearance. This fact does nothing to help his relationship with actual cats, who will still hate him in either his wild or dormant form. Usually a biped, the Lionthrope's fur bursts out from his face into a thick mane that you'd swear he had styled with a hair dryer. This werewolf is very fast and

good in a fight, though maybe not as willing a participant as other types. He'll never back down when he senses scared or wounded prey, but if he senses a worthy adversary, he may decide his advantage lies in his speed and will retreat and live to fight another day.

All of these types go through their transformations on the same dates, heal at the same speeds, hunt the same prey, and are dangerous in their own ways. While these werewolves possess different body types in their wild forms, there are no shared, distinguishing characteristics that manifest in their dormant forms.

CHAPTER SEVEN

Werewolf Dreams
and Stranger Things

I had one recurring dream, almost every night for a couple of weeks. Having that dream made those weeks the worst period of my life. I would spend all day worrying about going to sleep that night. It was like I was facing execution at the end of every day. I won't say too much about it to avoid triggering it again, but it involved me, my mom, a calico cat, and an electric carving knife.

—Jim O., Online Ad Buyer

Age: 41, Lyc age: 14

THE DREAMWORLD OF THE STAGE 1 LYCANTHROPE

Have you ever watched a sleeping dog suddenly twitch and flail its legs, and wondered what on earth that dog could be dreaming about? Well, you don't have to wonder anymore, because you're about to get a sneak peak.

The dreams of a recently bitten lycanthrope are so vivid, so terrifying, and so indescribably odd that they could only have been concocted in the mind of someone who is beginning to realize that they are part human and part bloodthirsty beast.

Invariably, during the first month after having been bitten, one of the major complaints of lycanthropes concerns their dreams and nightmares. The dreams feel so real and so inescapable that many lycanthropes worry they are descending into madness. It is not uncommon for many lycanthropes to experience long bouts of insomnia. They are so terrified by what is in store for them once they fall into a dream that the very thought of lying down for bed sends their hearts racing in a panic. Their fear of sleep is what keeps them up at night. Their fear of sleep is what keeps them up at night. Unfortunately, no matter what you do, the dreams and the nightmares are still going to come. This chapter can help you to cope with them.

Why Are My Dreams So Weird?

In the first month after you've been attacked by a werewolf, your entire physical makeup is undergoing drastic changes, and your mind is working overtime to try to make sense of it. When your mind is working harder, your dreams become more intense. You experience dreams so vivid that once you manage to shake yourself conscious, it will take far more than a pinch on the arm to convince yourself that you're really awake.

The closest comparison to a lycanthrope dream would be the kind of fever dream one experiences when fighting a viral infection and suffering through an excessively high body temperature. The body is fighting an invader in its bloodstream, and the mind is working hard to aid the fight—the intensity of the sleeper's dreams reflect this fight. The first stage of lycanthropy is akin to a viral infection, in that the lycantropin hormone is coursing through your blood for the first time and going to work on your molecular makeup. You are literally being transformed into an entirely new organism.

What Will I Dream About?

While the vividness of your dreams will be unparalleled, you might be far more disturbed by the subject matter of your dreams, which will be astoundingly strange. It is important to note that Stage 1 lycanthropes never report dreaming of themselves in werewolf or nonhuman form. This is because the newly bitten lycanthrope simply has no idea what exactly this form will take. Even if the lycanthrope is aware of his new nature, he can still only imagine his werewolf form using archetypes found in horror movies and novels. If a werewolf appears in a lycanthrope dream, it is usually being observed by the dreamer.

Some common lycanthrope dream types include:

Running. Lots and lots of running. Running for miles and miles with the feeling that you could keep running until the ends of the earth, on all gradations of terrain and in all kinds of weather. The feeling of this dream will be unmitigated joy.

Hunting. This dream usually involves the pursuit of a forest or farm animal, such as a deer or a sheep. You might be armed with a knife or a club (rarely a gun), or you might only be armed with your bare hands. While in the dream, the capture and kill of the prey will be experienced as a great accomplishment and with a great sense of fulfillment. After waking, however, the memory of the bloody and violent assault of your human form on a wild animal will be quite disturbing.

Gorging. The gorging dream can be very frightening to the sleeper, as it often seems as if you might never satisfy your hunger, that the dream might never end. You might sit down to an endless buffet of common foodstuffs, or you might find yourself in a vat of bloody, raw, red meat, which you will gnaw at and swallow voraciously.

The above are representative of the good dreams, or at least the moderately tolerable dreams, that a new lycanthrope can experience. Unfortunately, tolerable lycanthrope dreams are few and far between.

Why Are My Nightmares So Unbelievably Terrifying?

You are going to have nightmares. Your nightmares will be more frightening than any nightmare you have ever experienced. Your nightmares will be so frightening you'll worry that your life is in danger if you fall asleep.

It isn't.

Though your life is turning into something that you used to think only existed in nightmares, the nightmares you have in this new life are just as harmless as the nightmares you used to have when you were a child.

But way, way scarier.

Nightmares are your mind's way of dealing with stress and processing recent emotional or physical trauma. They are a common occurrence for sufferers of post-traumatic stress disorder, as the mind works hard to make sense of the overwhelming stimuli of a traumatic event.

Nightmares are also a way for your subconscious to warn

THOSE ARE 500-COUNT SHEETS!
PRECAUTIONS TO PREVENT SHREDDING
YOUR SHEETS OR YOUR PARTNER'S SKIN

Excessively vivid, violent dreams will cause you to thrash about in your bed just like that dog twitching and thrashing his legs. To prevent harming yourself or your bedding, you might consider wearing thick, protective workman's gloves to bed (Carhartt leather fencer gloves are ideal). You should also move all furniture away from the bed to avoid kicking your legs against a bedside lamp or chair and hurting your shin. Some lycanthropes have been known to wear shin guards to bed. If you find that your body thrashing during dreams is simply far too violent to be safe, you should consider sleeping with restraints securing your arms and legs to the bed, though this can often adversely affect your nightmares.

Additionally, if you sleep with a partner, you should seriously consider moving to a separate bed or bedroom during your first few months of lycanthropy. Your dreams will likely have you waking up in a panic several times a night, disturbing and worrying your partner, and your thrashing about could do your partner physical harm.

you that something is very wrong. While you may only have a vague sense of strange things being afoot, your subconscious is fully aware that something monumentally abnormal is taking place in your body, and it has decided it's time to go to DEFCON 1. Your nightmares are the only environment where your mind can fully express the urgency of what is at hand.

Some common lycanthrope nightmares include:

Violent murder of humans. Although the werewolf only kills to feed and to defend itself, your unconscious is recognizing your new instinct to hunt and kill. It has no context in which to incorporate these instincts, however, except for those contexts plucked from your human frame of reference. The resulting nightmares cast you as a psychotic, bloodthirsty killer of other humans. Lycanthropes have reported dreams in which they kill all varieties of acquaintances, loved ones, children and adults, mothers and fathers, wives and husbands. You will dream of killing by bludgeoning, stabbing, throttling, biting with your own teeth, and tearing apart with your bare hands. You will use hand-to-hand weapons. You will dream of feeding on those you kill, and all the while you will be aware of what you are doing, aware of the pleading screams of your victims as they implore you to let them be, but you will feel absolutely powerless to stop yourself.

Increasing violence and gore in dream imagery

Sexual exploration of animals and animal carcasses. Definitely one of the more confusing and disturbing of nightmares. Descriptions of these dreams go far beyond simple sexual intercourse between an animal and you. The scenario often involves treating the entire animal's body as a sexual organ, and you find yourself creating wounds in the animal's body with your fingernails and fists and feet, inserting your limbs into the wounds and exploring the tactile sensation of the innards. While the activity appears to be one of violence, this dream is invariably reported to have sexually aroused the dreamer, only to be followed by extreme disgust and terror upon waking.

Insect infestations. Lycanthropes report dreaming that their bodies and homes are swarming with insects such as ants, roaches, and bees, and there is no escape but to accept that you will soon be smothered by the swarm.

Chase. Completely unrelated to the hunting dream, the chase nightmare is common to lycanthropes and human alike. You are being chased, usually by predatory animals, the pursuers are closing in, and it is almost certain that you will be overtaken and mauled.

Car or vehicular trouble. You've lost control of your vehicle, whether it be a car, a plane, or a train, and you are trying to right the situation before you crash. In the dream you will also experience a perceived loss of motor skills in your body.

Being menaced by the dead. You will dream of deceased loved ones visiting you to do you physical harm or berate you with furious and obscene tirades.

I'm Just Gonna Try and Stay Awake for the Next Few Weeks

The nightmares can get so bad that staying awake for weeks on end will feel like a more desirable option. This is a terrible idea. Going without sleep for excessive periods of time can only lead to madness. Worst of all, you will reach a state where you are unsure whether you are sleeping or conscious, bringing your dream state closer to crossing the line into your waking world. Ultimately, you will fall asleep again, and when you do, your dreams will be even more vivid and more intense.

As far as the dreams getting better after the change, this is not quite true. They don't exactly get "better," but they do get different, and far easier to cope with.

Dream Therapy Exercises to Take Control of a Recurring Nightmare

While nothing can be done to stop the nightmares, there are exercises you can do to control them.

SLEEPING PILLS ARE NO BETTER THAN SLEEP DEPRIVATION

While sleeping pills can prevent you from having dreams (or at least from remembering them), they are not recommended for werewolves. Your system is too strong to be affected by a typical sleeping pill dosage, and you'll have to ingest far more pills than recommended. Even if you do take enough, you'll eventually build up a tolerance and require a larger dose. After using sleeping pills for a stretch, when you finally go without them, the dreams you'll have will be all the more vivid and terrifying, as if they've been building up and finally burst through the door you'd kept them locked behind.

Imagery Rehearsal

This is a good exercise for defusing a recurring nightmare. It involves taking the scenario of the nightmare, imagining a different way for the nightmare to play out, and then rehearsing that new scenario in your mind.

For example, let's say you have a recurring nightmare in which you chase after a terrified young child and then, when you apprehend the child, you crush his skull against a rock and feed on his brain matter. With imagery rehearsal, you would concoct a new way for the dream to play out. You might imagine chasing the child until the child comes upon a waiting hot-air balloon, manned by a pleasant-seeming elderly man in a jeff cap. The elderly man sets the balloon afloat just as you come around the bend to watch the boy escape. With imagery rehearsal, you would write down this new sce-

Rehearse a happy ending

nario, and you would spend time rehearsing the scenario in your mind, imagining yourself in the dream: chasing the child, coming into the field too late, and then finding the child rising up in the sky in a beautiful hot-air balloon and waving down at you alongside a kindly old man. Rehearsing this scenario will plant the plot in your mind should the dream occur again, and you might be surprised to find your new, rehearsed ending is the path the nightmare takes from then on.

Lucid Dream Exercises

Nothing defuses the power of a dream like the realization that the dream isn't real. There are exercises that can train you to respond to a nightmare by determining that you are in fact dreaming. Keep a dream journal to become more familiar with the nature and details of your recurring dreams, and perform "reality checks" throughout your waking life to determine that you are really awake. These can include asking yourself things like, "Do things make sense presently?" or, "Could I fly if I wanted to?" Turning on light switches several times and seeing if they work is also a reality check. If you do this during your waking life, you're likely to do it during your dreams as well, and you will soon be able to know when a nightmare is just a dream.

TRUE LEGENDS?

IF YOU DIE IN A DREAM, YOU CAN'T DIE IN REAL LIFE, BUT IF YOU KILL IN A DREAM, YOU CAN KILL IN REAL LIFE

A Stage 1 lycanthrope just a week away from her first Moon was having a terrible nightmare. In the nightmare she was playing fetch with a golden retriever. When the dog came back, the lyc ripped one of the dog's legs off his body and tossed it. The dog ran on his other three legs to fetch its fourth. When the dog brought the leg back to the woman, she bit one of the dog's ears off and spat it a hundred yards. The dog raced to grab the ear in its mouth and returned it to the woman. Then the woman proceeded to rip the dog's tail from its body, then another leg, then its penis, then an eyeball, each time making the dog chase after its body parts and return them to the woman, until finally the dog was left with only one leg. That's when the woman dug her fingernails into the dog's belly and tore it open wide enough to bury her head inside and feed on the dog's intestines.

When the woman finally woke up from her nightmare, she was choking for air and couldn't see. She fell from the bed and threw up onto her bedroom floor. When she could finally see again she realized she was covered in blood. She then peered up onto the bed and saw that her husband was dead, his stomach torn open and his insides caved in where her face had just been burrowing.

A NOTE ON ENCOUNTERS WITH THE UNDEAD

You might start seeing ghosts.

Numerous werewolves report having been visited by ghosts or spirits of the dead during their early stages of lycanthropy. We include this as a subsection of this chapter since many find it difficult to say definitively whether the spiritual encounter was a dream, a trick of a rattled lycanthrope mind, or an actual visit from the deceased. This should not be confused with encounters with vampires, a group of the undead who are very real and very hard to avoid, no matter what stage of lycanthropy you are in. (See Chapter 20, "The Trouble with Vampires.")

If you've gotten loose and attacked someone, you may

encounter a spirit in the form of one of your victims, or in the form of a relative or loved one whose death particularly affected you. We will not go so far as to state that these spirits are real or a dream. What we can say with certitude is that, be it a vision, dream, flashback, symptom of an undisclosed ailment, or bona fide supernatural encounter, the experience of seeing and interacting with deceased friends, loved ones, and/or victims of werewolf attacks is almost universally reported as a pretty big downer. It's a shock to see them, they usually look mutilated or excessively decomposed, and in many instances they harangue you to kill yourself.

Still, if you see a ghost, it is important to remember they can't really do anything to you.

What is at first frightening will soon grow tedious

As spectral beings, they can scold, berate, and jump out at you, but even if they look like shambling, disgusting zombies, their bark is worse than their bite. In the dozens of documented brushes with the spirit world, there has never been a recorded instance of any ghost ever being able to touch or harm the lycanthrope he was haunting.

Watch out for lying. Always listen to what a ghost says, but take it with a grain of salt. If it is the ghost of someone you killed while in your wild state, they could have a beef against you and, as a result, come up with some pretty outlandish ways of convincing you to kill yourself. Sticks and stones. One longtime lycanthrope wrote of a ghost of a victim appearing to him and claiming to have seen the future. As the ghost told it, if the lycanthrope didn't commit suicide immediately, he would rape and kill his own mother during his next Moon. Even if the absurdity of this claim wasn't immediately apparent (a werewolf has almost no sexual desire in his wild state), this rather lazy lie was exposed by the fact that the mother in question had died a decade prior. As when dealing with information garnered from the living, it's wise to consider the source.

Why all this talk of suicide? A visit from a spirit, especially when it's the ghost of one of your victims, will often involve the spirit pleading with you to take measures to protect future victims from the danger you pose. Invariably, the spirit will tell you that taking your own life is the only way to be sure you won't harm another.

The suggestion of suicide in these encounters is a strong argument for these visits being entirely the product of an anxious, guilt-plagued lycanthrope mind. In the early stages, lycanthropes are absolutely terrified of what they're capable of, and if they've killed, their guilt will naturally lead them to thoughts of ending it all. Certainly lots of these encounters with ghosts can be explained by the frantic brain activity of the Stage 1 lycanthrope, not to mention reports of lycantropin sometimes having a hallucinogenic effect on the recently bitten. But considering the frequency of the encounters and the vividness of the visions, perhaps not all of them can be explained as simple tricks of the mind.

This is another good time to remind you that, morals aside, the killing of human beings is a terrible idea, for your dreams and mental health alone. Throughout all of our research, reading, and interviews, we have never encountered even one instance of a lycanthrope being visited by the ghost of a thirty-pound bag of dog food or the phantoms of recently deceased livestock.

PART TWO

LIVING, LOVING, AND LEARNING . . . WITH LYCANTHROPY

CHAPTER EIGHT

Home Is Where You Hang Your Restraint System

I have been all over. I'm lucky enough not to be limited by my financial means. I've lived in New York and Paris. Perth and Siberia. Lima, Peru, and Okinawa, Japan. I've lived in castles, huts, and fortified bunkers. Of all the places I have lived, all the exotic locales and soaring cities, the magnificent homes and the ultra-modern fortresses, for my money there is no better home for a werewolf than in my current place of residence: South Orange, New Jersey.

All the provisions I need are a short drive away. I reside in a nice two-floor house with a large basement. Pleasant neighbors. Not too nosy.

South Orange. It's a real werewolf town.

—Name and occupation withheld,
South Orange, NJ, resident
Age: 59, Lyc age: 35

WHERE SHOULD WEREWOLVES LIVE?

Everyone hates moving, but a werewolf requires a pretty specific living situation. In order to avoid being discovered, you need privacy and the space to have your Moons without any nosy neighbors poking about. This chapter offers a shortlist of ideal conditions for a lycanthrope's place of residence, as well as conditions and amenities to avoid. We will also grade types of locale according to how amenable they are to the needs and wants of a modern werewolf.

IDEAL LIVING CONDITIONS

When looking for a new home, you should pick a locale that offers the following:

- Privacy
- Spaciousness
- Access to brand-name retail goods (big-box retailers)
- A violent crime rate that is slightly above average, but still well below your nation's top ten most violent cities
- Typical desirable living amenities (decent schools, good air quality, low property taxes)

Privacy

Privacy might be a lycanthrope's most important asset. You need to live someplace where people generally keep to themselves and neighborly curiosity is at a minimum. You want to be where neighbors don't necessarily know one another by first name and won't grow suspicious if they spot you toting all sorts of chains, straps, and construction materials into your home.

Spaciousness

Spaciousness often goes hand-in-hand with privacy. You should try to reside in an area where it's economically feasible to live alone (no roommates) and, if possible, where you can live in a single-occupancy house (no row homes with shared walls if you can avoid it). A house with a basement (especially windowless) is ideal. With a house, you have the option of fortifying your space and enduring your Moons with maximum privacy.

Being a homeowner beats apartment living hands down. You can make as much noise as you like, and if you have a

---

SORRY, YOU'RE BUSY THAT DAY

December 24, 2015:

Cancel those plans to wait up for Santa this year. If you bump into old Saint Nick on Christmas Eve 2015, that's the night before a full moon, and it won't be milk and cookies you'll be hungry for.

---

basement, you can fortify it without having your living space dominated by cages and chains. Even if you manage to fortify an apartment without drawing the attention of a landlord or neighbors with noisy renovations, you still have to worry about neighbors hearing your growling and struggling during a Moon and calling the police with a report that their neighbor is keeping a wild animal as a pet.

Additionally, owning a single-occupancy house is very different from owning an apartment. The owner of an apartment will more than likely have to clear any renovations with a co-op board (there exists no more invasive a governing body when it comes to seeking privacy within your dwelling), while the owner of a house can make all variety of interior renovations as long as they adhere to local zoning codes.

Access to Quality Retail Goods

Whether you're fortifying your basement or strapping yourself down for your Moons, you need a lot of supplies. You need hardware, metals, durable strapping, and portable coolers for raw meat storage. Most everything you need to prepare for your Moon can be found at big-box retailers, especially Wal-Mart and Home Depot. In many American towns, these stores are often located in the same shopping center, and you can finish your shopping without moving your car from its parking space. Big cities and very small towns

Be near strip malls and "big-box" retailers

tend to lack these sorts of retailers, however, and you can be forced to visit numerous specialty shops or rely on mail order. You should use mail order to replace items in advance or to purchase duplicate items, but when it comes to preparing for a Moon, time is of the essence. It's best to visit a brick-and-mortar retailer so you can walk out of the store with provisions in hand. The closer you live to big-box retail stores, the better.

A Violent Crime Rate That Is Slightly Above Average

If you ever get loose, chances are that you will murder a human or animal in your immediate vicinity. In towns that go months if not years without a single assault on their police blotter, your attack can incite a panic and force the town's police force to devote all of their manpower to apprehending the perpetrator. This is obviously very dangerous for you.

For this reason, you want to live someplace where a single violent crime does not immediately hit the front page of the

CSI CAN ALWAYS CATCH THEIR GUY

In the wake of an attack on a human, it's important to remember that whether you are in your wild or dormant form, your DNA is the same. It has been significantly altered since you've been bitten, but it does not change again when you transform from dormant to wild. In short, if the police collect a hair follicle at the crime scene, a DNA comparison will match that werewolf follicle to a sample taken from your human head. Though witnesses and pathologists might send the police looking for a wild animal, if the investigation comes down to DNA and alibis, you can be implicated.

newspaper. A moderate to above-moderate level of violent crime is most desirable. You want a community that has a high enough murder rate that one mysterious killing won't start a panic. But you don't want the murder rate to be so high that homicide detectives are experienced enough to know at first glance that they are dealing with an exceptional (and likely not-entirely-human) suspect, and are creative and diligent enough that they might follow the trail to your doorstep.

Typical Desirable Living Amenities

In addition to the concerns over dealing with an experienced homicide squad, a town with an exceptionally high murder rate is not desirable for the obvious reason: It's dangerous. While the above conditions address the concerns of a werewolf, keep in mind that you must live in your dormant state for the majority of your life. To that end, your concerns over the simple wants and needs are as valid as those of every other human on this planet. Good schools, low taxes—these are as essential to your well-being as strong cages and durable restraints. A Realtor can answer most of the questions you may have about a potential neighborhood, and more information can be obtained with a little Internet research.

RECOMMENDED LOCALES

Taking the above conditions into consideration, the following locales are ranked from most to least amenable as a place of residence for the modern lycanthrope:

Suburbs and Exurbs

Grade: A
Suburbs and so-called "exurbs" (towns within commuting distance of major cities that have flourished due to people being unable to afford to reside in the cities where they work) offer privacy, spaciousness, access to major retail establishments, a moderate level of violent crime, and a decent quality of life.

Suburbs might be the most desirable, as they are usually immediately adjacent to major cities and so possess many of the same amenities as cities, with the added bonus of space

---

HEY WOLFMAN, MOW YOUR DAMN LAWN!

The biggest mistake a suburban or exurban lycanthrope can make is failing to be a good neighbor. In the 'burbs, your neighbors are more than happy to pay you no mind as long as you keep your lawn mowed and take down your Christmas lights not long after New Year's. Once you become an eyesore to the neighborhood, all eyes will turn to you. Simply make sure your house looks like everyone else's and you won't have the head of the block association knocking on your door to complain about your sidewalk not being shoveled on a night when you happen to be chained to your basement wall.

and privacy. However, these suburban areas are often not very affordable, as they are the preferred place of residence for many well-to-do professionals with families.

Due to the rising cost of living in American cities, there are many more **exurban** neighborhoods that offer affordable housing. Due to their sudden growth, these neighborhoods are increasingly being catered to by major retailers. The violent crime rate in these areas might be lower than the national average, but if a single-occupancy suburban home is beyond your means, an exurban neighborhood might be your best bet.

Cities

Grade: B-
Urban locales simultaneously offer the best and worst conditions for privacy. In the big city, everyone generally prefers

Apartment living is far from ideal

to keep to themselves. Unfortunately, everyone is also living on top of one another, and if a neighbor feels you are infringing on his privacy by, say, making loud renovations or terrifying growling noises, he will confront you. If you live in the city, you will most likely be forced to endure your Moons out-of-home, in remote or run-down areas of the city or a rented safe room out of town, if you can afford it. In-house transformation is next to impossible. On the plus side, if you ever attack somebody, it's not likely to raise an eyebrow, and you will never draw suspicion for curious behavior while in your dormant state.

DON'T BELIEVE IT!
COMMUNITY TOLERANCE FOR LYCANTHROPES

There has never been any known situation in which a community learned of a werewolf living in their midst and came to tolerate and even embrace the werewolf as some sort of "extra-special neighbor." Some films or novels will tell a tale of a lycanthrope who comes clean to his neighbors and then impresses upon them the precautions he takes to ensure their safety, and his neighbors end up trusting him and even protecting him. Other stories might depict the denizens of a village all huddling together in a bar or a basement during a full moon, suffering the night together while the werewolf they know lives among them roams the hillside slaughtering sheep or unsuspecting travelers.

DON'T BELIEVE IT! Try to remember your way of thinking before you were bitten. If you found out that a werewolf lived in your neighborhood, you and your neighbors would surely do everything you could to drive that werewolf away or worse. You wouldn't accept any reassurances, and you wouldn't just huddle in a crowd someplace three times a month while a killer beast ravaged your town. You'd kill the wolf if you had to, and that's exactly what your neighbors will do if they find you out. Keep it secret.

Rustic, Underdeveloped Areas

Grade: C

Many a lycanthrope has chosen to pack up and go live in a cabin someplace in the woods. While this is not for everybody, it does provide you with privacy (in some cases, you can be miles from the nearest neighbor while surrounded by free-roaming forest animals) and spaciousness. You, of course, have little to no access to retail establishments, but as your chances of being discovered decrease, so does your need for provisions. Depending on your disposition, however, your quality of life might be all but nonexistent, not to mention the

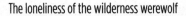

The loneliness of the wilderness werewolf

learning curve you'll have to ascend if you've lived in the city all your life. Choosing this type of residence is akin to deciding you're a wild animal and must live like one. If you love the outdoors and have been looking for an excuse to become a woodsman, by all means go find your cabin. But the rustic life is not for everyone.

Rural Locales

Grade: C-/D+

Small, agricultural towns or poor rural areas might be the least desirable for a lycanthrope. You have little to no access to major retailers, the town's population is usually so small that everyone knows everybody's business, and the slightest odd behavior can get people talking. Worst of all, a violent assault or murder can instigate a lynch mob. Hollywood movies may be wrong about a lot of things, but the whole "mob of ignorant villagers with pitchforks and torches" thing is right on the money. And in this day and age, they have guns. The best thing about these areas is spaciousness, but they have little else to offer a lycanthrope.

CLIMATE

A moderate climate is ideal for the lycanthrope. While most precautions are taken to avoid getting loose during a Moon, there must also be precautions for what to do when it happens. When you change back into your dormant state, you will be naked and unconscious, and might remain that way for up to fifteen hours. Subzero winters and hot desert climates can be lethal in these situations. One of the major causes of lycanthrope death is post-Moon exposure to the elements.

DON'T BELIEVE IT!
"DAY CHASERS":
THE NEVER-ENDING JOURNEY
OF THE MIGRATORY LYCANTHROPE

The connection between the werewolf's transformation and the full moon can be explained by the high level of iron in a lycanthrope's blood, which makes his biochemistry more sensitive to the moon's phases, instigating a surge of lycantropin around the time of the full moon. However, many lycanthropes believe that this biochemical cause is responsible only for the early Moons of a werewolf's life, and in later years the werewolf's mental anticipation of the coming Moon is what causes the lycantropin surge. They believe the werewolf's changes are set to a kind of mental-biological clock. Some lycanthropes have tried to manipulate that clock.

Day chasers are werewolves with unlimited financial means who have taken to a migratory lifestyle. Since werewolves only transform after nightfall, day chasers believe that living in extreme latitudes that experience months without nightfall can keep a lycanthrope's changes at bay. They think that they can trick their bodies into behaving as though the full moon isn't coming. Day chasers will spend the entirety of their summers at the northernmost points of the globe (Alaska, Iceland). In the winter, they head as far south as they can, without hitting Antarctica, to places like Punta Arenas, Chile, where the night can be reduced to just a few hours of darkness. Legend has it that some day chasers have gone months without a Moon or have shortened the duration of their Moons to just a few manageable hours at a time.

DON'T BELIEVE IT!

While there have been accounts of this tactic working, they are likely urban legend or involve older werewolves who don't transform as often anymore. The body's mental-biological clock will come into sync with the locale and instigate a change, even though it might still appear to be daylight. No matter how light it might be outside, the moon's phase is not affected, and if your mental clock begins to perceive a certain segment of the day as "nighttime," it will spark the change. If you have the means to be migratory, you should take the proper precautions to restrain yourself during your Moon.

CHAPTER NINE

A Safe Room of One's Own

He knew he had me in that divorce. Had me by the short tufts. I couldn't ask for a damn thing. All he had to do to shut me up was threaten to put the house on the table. Twenty-one years I labored over that basement. Secure as a bank vault. He knew I'd never give it up. So he got the cars, the kids, half our bank accounts, and half my earnings for the next twenty years. But I kept the house. And my beautiful safe room.

—Elizabeth K., Public Works Architect

Age: 55, Lyc age: 23

A werewolf needs a home. You should always have a predesignated "safe room" where you'll sequester yourself every month to have your Moons. This should be a space where there are no surprises, no chance of anyone wandering in unawares. It should be secure enough that no one can get in and, most importantly, that *you* can't get out.

Safe rooms vary depending on where you live and what your financial means are. Here's a list and review of the various types of safe rooms, some less accessible than others:

BOMB SHELTERS

There are few places as ideal to change into a werewolf as a bomb shelter. Bomb shelters are underground, ensuring that no one will hear your howling and growling. They're secure enough to withstand a nuclear blast, so they'll definitely be

Deep underground, no one can hear you howl

impenetrable to any curious neighbors. They're designed to have everything you could need to live there for many weeks, so they make a nice place to camp out for just a couple of nights a month. The point of entry will be intricate enough that you won't just be able to shove your way out once you're wild. If you have the funds and the land on which to dig, a bomb shelter cannot be beat.

PANIC ROOMS

Basically, the rich man's above-ground bomb shelter, but far more high-tech. These in-home fortified rooms are virtually impenetrable from the outside. Once you're inside, you won't be able to get out without entering a predetermined code into a keypad (when you're wild, your intelligence will be about at the level of a relatively smart dog, so you won't even know what numbers are, let alone remember keypad number combinations). Most of these rooms allow for monitoring what's going on outside as well, so when your Moon has passed, before stepping back outside you can check to make sure there isn't a terrified mob waiting with pitchforks. Extremely expensive, but worth if it you can afford one.

A CAGE AND A COW

A less extravagant alternative is the simple in-house zoo cage, stocked with a live cow (or similarly satisfying animal; check the meal chart on page 113). The cage should be composed of pure steel, and it should be the size of your standard tiger cage at the zoo. When you've turned wild, you won't possess the faculties to know how to put a key in a lock and get out of that cage, and if you have enough to eat, you might not even want to. Just make sure to hide the key within reach outside of the cage, for when you change back to dormant form.

YOUR BASEMENT

If you have your own house with a basement, there is no reason why you can't renovate that space for your Moons. Basements are underground, which makes them ideal for containing noise and keeping out of sight of peeping neighbors. You'll need to seal up any windows with cement brick, and you'll need to line the walls with sound-proofing tiles or eggcrate-style foam padding. A thick steel door will be necessary for the entrance, and you might want to double that up with a steel security gate. A complicated lock or several latches and padlocks will be necessary so that you can lock yourself in and be sure you won't get out. When wild, you won't know how to operate door locks, so your only method of escape will be to crash through the door. You want to make sure the lock is complex enough that you won't be able to jar yourself free.

WORKING LATE?

Excerpt from interview with Manuel E., Home Appraiser
Age 50, Lyc age: 10

I got cocky. Or maybe just greedy. I took two contracts on the day of my Moon, giving me only about an hour to drive back home and lock up. I was speeding pretty good and must have been plenty distracted, because I didn't see the cat running in front of my car until there was nothing for me to do but swerve out of the way. The cat lived, but my car went straight into a tree, impaling one of the tires on the crunched bumper. It was not gonna get me home.

I jumped from the car and grabbed my backup bag from the trunk, then took off running. I wasn't even sure what neighborhood I was in. In my bag I had about twenty feet of chain link, a few combo padlocks, manacles, a change of clothes, and this muzzling gag that I hadn't really tried out yet. I was looking for anything, an industrial site, a warehouse, a school basement. If I even found a Dumpster I could have locked myself up inside it. But there was nothing but suburban homes for blocks and blocks. I knew I was screwed, and if I was gonna lock myself away I had to pick someplace right there to do it. That's when I looked down and found my spot.

The sewer.

No choice. I got down on the ground and lifted the lid off the curbside drain. I shoved my bag down and then slid in after it, dropping about ten feet and landing on the bag. I didn't even get a chance to put on any chains or manacles or anything, because the next thing I remember I was waking up near what I thought was a waterfall. I was on this rock wall, and all this water was pouring down from the street drain above me. I was nude and freezing cold. I managed to trace my way back to where I started by following a trail of chewed-up rat bones and my droppings from the night before. I finally found my bag and put on my spare clothes, and then I found a ladder that led up to one of the open curb drains.

When I got back to my car it had already been towed. I made sure to call in sick for my second Moon so I could get nice and snug in my safe room several hours in advance.

Obviously, if you have your washer and dryer or any other appliances down there, you'll need to cage those up as well to protect them from being damaged when you start throwing your wolf weight around.

The ideal basement space has a concrete floor with a storm drain at its shallowest point. When you eat during your Moon, it will get messy, especially if you're feeding on live animals. Being able to just hose the floor down the next day can be very handy.

Necessary renovations to the space will cost you far less than a bomb shelter, but it will still require an investment of one or two thousand dollars, depending on how much needs to be done.

RETAIL/OFFICE SPACE

If you live in an apartment or a small house and fortifying/sound-proofing for a safe room isn't feasible, it can be very cheap and practical to rent retail/office space in a small industrial complex and fortify that space for your Moons.

While renting a storefront in a busy shopping center or mini-mall won't work for you, there are many smaller retail complexes with just a handful of storefront units being used for medical and legal practices and notaries, all of them shutting their doors promptly at 6 p.m. These smaller complexes can be a ghost town at night, leaving you all by your lonesome to have your Moon. The rent is usually far cheaper than renting an apartment, since the space is usually relatively barebones and not intended for use as a residence. The cheaper of these units will probably have fewer windows and doors to deal with too.

MINI-STORAGE UNITS

If you don't have a basement or room in your home to fortify for your Moons, renting a mini-storage space is an option. This is risky, but if you know the mini-storage location's rules of operation well, you can feel relatively safe here.

Not all mini-storage locations are open twenty-four hours. You need to pick one that closes its doors early in the evening, and that has limited security patrols of the grounds overnight. In many mini-storage complexes, the long-term, larger units will be in a separate area of the lot, farther away from the more heavily trafficked units. You can rent one of these long-term units, arrive before closing, lock yourself in, and have your Moon in privacy.

Before using one of these units for your Moon, though, you should test it out on several other nights of the month. Show up, lock yourself in, and make lots of noise throughout the night. If after three or four different nights no one comes poking around, the unit should be doable for your Moon.

Famous Lycs Through Time

Sir Francis Drake, Explorer (1540–95, Lyc yrs: 1578–95) During his famous ocean journey around the world from 1577–80, he was bitten in port at Argentina. When he finally returned to England and reported to Queen Elizabeth, he blamed his dramatically decimated crew on scurvy.

ABANDONED INDUSTRIAL SPACES

If your budget is limited and you have no basement or similar space, you should go find an abandoned industrial space and see if you can turn it into your own private clubhouse. Old factories or office buildings can be full of raw space and sturdy structures upon which you can restrain yourself. If they've been left abandoned, they're probably in a part of town where no one's complaining about the eyesore, which means you'll be alone. You do run the risk of sharing the space with the homeless or teens looking for a place to drink, but if they even hear you growl just once, chances are they'll figure out a way to get away from you before laying eyes on you.

WIDE-OPEN SPACES

If you live near a desert or mountains, you can head out into that no-man's-land and chain yourself up outdoors for a Moon. It's important that you stay clear of common camping and hunting areas. And just because you're out in the wild, that doesn't mean you get to behave like a wild animal. Restraints are important. If you just roam free you can wake up the next day miles from where you started. No need to be overly cautious with the restraints; you can give yourself enough leeway to perhaps secure yourself a little free-range dinner. While you'll probably make enough noise to keep animals at bay, you might get lucky and catch one.

PRECAUTIONS

Get there early. Always visit your safe room the day before your first Moon of the month and get there very early the day of your Moon. You want there to be no surprises when you get there. If you show up just before your change and find that someone broke the lock on your door, you will have very little time to secure the space before nightfall.

Always have a backup. Even if your safe room is in your basement or on your property, you should always have a backup in case unforeseeable circumstances force you to change elsewhere. You should scope out those abandoned industrial spaces on the outskirts of town and keep some restraints in the trunk of your car in case you need to get there in a hurry.

Keep everything up to code. If you're building on your own property, be sure to obey zoning codes within your township. You don't want to draw the attention of city inspectors who have been tipped off by neighbor complaints about construction noise. "What's he building in there?" is a question that people don't shake from their heads very easily.

Vary your route. If you commute to your safe room, you don't want lyc hunters to track you there. (Read more about werewolf hunters in Chapter 22, "Werewolf Hunters.") Additionally, if you're having your Moon at an abandoned industrial space or someplace else where you're not supposed to be, park some distance away from the space. You don't want to alert patrolling police officers that someone might be trespassing and they should take a look around.

Prepare for if you get loose. Our best intentions sometimes fail us, and even the most state-of-the-art safe room designs can be cracked by a hungry werewolf. There are additional precautions you can take to mitigate the dangers of getting loose:

• *If possible, replace stairs with ladders.* Whether it's your own basement or a bomb shelter, an underground safe room is ideal. If possible, outfit your safe room with a ladder instead of a staircase. In your wild state, you can climb stairs and on occasion even trees, but you won't have the coordination necessary to make the ascent, rung by rung, up a ladder.

• *Near the entryway, outside the door, leave some foodstuffs laced with tranquilizers.* You'll hopefully gobble that down before taking off and, with any luck, pass out before you even make it to the street. Drugging yourself during your Moon is not recommended, but this is of course only a case of last resort.

• *Rig a trap of strong rope netting.* When you leave your safe room and you trip the trigger, the netting will hopefully tangle you in its grasp before you get away.

• *Double up as many safeguards as you can.* If there is an entranceway to the safe room, be sure that the door is steel and bolted, as well. If the safe room entrance connects to your home, outfit your ground floor windows with bars or steel shutters and put a steel security gate over your front and back doors. Whenever you have the means, you should always consider adding additional fortification. When it comes to a werewolf getting loose, each additional obstacle could be the difference between a close call and a rampage.

TOP 10 WORST PLACES TO BE DURING A MOON

10. In a movie theater

9. On a commercial passenger flight

8. Driving

7. Hosting a children's sleepover

6. On a military base

5. In jail

4. In a hospital

3. In a mall

2. On a cruise

1. Piccadilly Circus or Times Square

CHAPTER TEN

Strapping In

The rule of thumb is to go three sizes up. If you wear pants with a 34 waist, your wolf waist is a 40. If you wear a 17 neck, it's jumping up to 20. After your Moon you can see what's torn and what's stretched and let it out some for next time, but that's pretty much the guesstimate.

—Lionel B., Seller of Bondage Fetish Wear
and Werewolf Restraint Suits
Age: 40, Lyc age: 19

Locking yourself up in a durable safe room is more than adequate for keeping yourself from getting loose. But for that extra security to guarantee you won't get anywhere, you might consider a good, strong restraint system.

Picking the right restraint system takes careful consideration. If you pick a system that is too constrictive, it could lead to injury or fatality. Alternately, restraining the wrong part of the body has led some werewolves to chew through their own limbs in order to get free.

Don't rush into the wrong restraints. If you can lock yourself away for a Moon or two, you can conduct some experiments that will give you an idea of your ballpark werewolf size.

DESIGNING YOUR OWN RESTRAINT SYSTEM

There is no one right way to strap in for your Moon, but there are a great many wrong ways:

Wrong Ways

Making the restraints too tight. You'll be growing to almost double your human size. If the restraints are too tight, you can either choke or restrict blood flow to your limbs.

Using unsheathed chains. The kinks of chains can pinch and tear at the skin, especially after eight hours of violent wriggling. You could change back to find a gaping open wound in your torso. Only use chains covered with a rubber or plastic sheath.

Collaring the neck only. On your first try, you stand a good chance of choking yourself if the collar is too small. If it's too big, you'll slip out of it in no time. You also stand a good chance of ripping the base up with a jerk of your neck. If you can imagine a junkyard dog running fast enough to tear the stake of its chain from the ground, imagine how durable the base would have to be to hold a three-hundred-pound wolf.

Chaining the wrists to a base. If just your wrists are bound to a base and you can reach your mouth to your wrist, you might try to chew off your paws to escape. Remember, in your wild state you won't be thinking, "Darnit, I can't hunt now." You'll be thinking, "I am presently defenseless against predators and must break free or die."

Binding the limbs together. Not recommended. Handcuffs work on a human because if you struggle too much, you'll incur pain. When in your wild state, you'll keep struggling through the pain, doing whatever you can to get free. When you change back, you might find the skin under your restraints rubbed clean to the bone. While transformation involves breakdown and regeneration of tissue, your body can't regenerate what's been torn away and is sitting in a pool of blood at your feet.

Recommended Placement of Restraints

Restraining the torso is the best way to hold a werewolf. Chains or straps should go over your shoulders, under your armpits, around your waist, and down around the crotch. The multiple positioning of straps prevents you from localizing your captivity to any one part of the body. It also prevents you from being able to yank the base from the wall, floor, or ceiling by jerking your body. Further, this allows you enough freedom to feed on any meat or livestock that you've provided for yourself.

| Wrong | Wrong | Right |

Recommended Materials

Straps. You should use the same kind of utility straps, usually nylon or polyester, that are used for tying down cargo. You can purchase them at boating stores, lumber yards, or larger hardware stores such as Home Depot. If they can hold a boat to a trailer or a pile of logs on a flatbed, they'll be able to hold you when you're wild. Cargo straps are rated for how much weight they can hold without buckling. You'll want straps rated to one thousand pounds. Salesmen can also help you purchase winches and buckles that will lock the straps into place. You should request binding that has some give, but that retracts with the shifting of weight.

Many cargo-hold systems are very advanced, and they work in much the same way as your restraints should. When a pile of lumber is rumbling down the highway on the back of a truck, that pile of logs is straining and struggling against the restraints the same way you will be, and the restraint system responds in kind. Where the pressure is the greatest, the restraints give just enough to keep from snapping, while retracting in other areas where there is no struggle. Ideally, this is how your restraints should work.

Sheathed chains. Sheathed chains are made of chain link with plastic or rubber sheathing to protect the skin from pinching. Steel chains are good and durable, and many lycs prefer them to straps, simply because steel offers some a sense of security that fabric straps cannot. But you must use sheathed chains. Those kinks can rip you apart in ways you wouldn't think possible.

Suiting fabric. To further protect the skin you can wear a form-fitting bodysuit. A good fabric to use is the kind of neoprene and spandex polyblend that is used for many wet suits. These suits are great for durability, and the spandex component allows them to stretch around the growing body (though you should still purchase it three sizes too big). Your chains and straps can either be fitted on the outside of the suit, or you can sew them into the fabric.

How to Tell How Big You Get

There's always video of course, but we caution against any video documentation unless it's absolutely necessary and hastily destroyed after viewing. And when it comes to sizing, video will still make you rely on your eye. There are more reliable, far safer methods to get your wild size down.

Elastic neckbands. Your neck size should increase by about three sizes. So to get a good sense of your werewolf neck size, cut the elastic neckband out of a T-shirt three sizes too big for you and wear it around your neck in advance of your Moon. After you change back, check the neckband. If it ripped at the seam, it was too small. If it doesn't seem to have been stretched at all, it was too big. Somewhere in between those two options will give you a good idea of your neck size.

Store-bought denim shorts. Again, go three sizes too big. Slip into the oversized shorts before your Moon, belting them with a shoelace or something else that will easily tear. You want the pants to stay on while you're writhing around during the change, but you don't want to belt them, since you don't know your size yet, and a too-tight belt could do damage.

If you simply grow too big to fit into the jeans, the seams will break before you hurt yourself. After you change back, you'll check those seams to see which of them were torn and which held firm. That should give you a good gauge of your waist, thighs, and crotch.

The Base

Once you've got your bonds positioned on your body, they have to be anchored to a base. We recommend a base with several equidistant points of restraint, if possible. If all of your

---

DON'T BELIEVE IT!
STRAITJACKETS DON'T WORK

Though better than handcuffs, the straitjacket is far from effective. The tough duck-cloth canvas material of an institutional straitjacket might be hard for a human to tear, but with your claws you won't have the same trouble in your wild state. Further, before you manage to rip through the sleeves, your hands will be placed in such a way that your claws might end up tearing into your own body first.

---

restraints are bound to just one point, you could eventually yank the base free. With several points, lunging and jerking in one direction might strain one of the points but will put no strain on another. Since you're only wild for approximately eight hours, you will likely not have time to pull all of your points of restraint free. A multiple point base can be created by using the cleats that are fitted to boat docks. You can install these cleats around your safe room. They should be screwed to studs in your wall or ceiling, or into your floor.

You can also drive approximately thirty-inch-long eyelet screws through your ceiling or through the stud of a wall. The screws should come out the other end to allow you to bolt them in place. Then you can run your chains or straps through the eyelets.

If you are looking for something already installed that you can bind yourself to, you can try a heating pipe, but only if the pipe runs out the floor and into the ceiling, and if there is no joint visible at the point where you're strapping yourself. You don't want to be able to tear the pipe at the joint or bend it free.

Muzzling

Some lycanthropes worry about the noise they'll make in their wild state. If you don't want the neighbors to hear a lot of howling or growling, you can try outfitting yourself with a muzzle or gag, but this can require a great deal of trial and error—and also prohibit you from feeding during your Moon, which is not recommended. Starving yourself in your wild state can cause you to be even more hostile than normal, and the effects of starvation (fatigue, dehydration) will be evident when you return to your dormant state, but if noise is a top concern of yours, you might have no choice. (For more on proper diet, see Chapter 11, "Diet and Livestock.")

Muzzling is extremely difficult, but there have been some designs that have shown mild success. The sock is one.

The Sock

The sock was designed by a developer of leathers in Helsinki, Finland, in 1977. It is a kind of rubberized leather wind-sock that fits around the back of the head, with several tough rubber straps over the top of the skull and an open-ended tube of leather dangling from the front of the face. You pull it on before your change, and as you transform, your snout should extend through the tube of the sock, which will cling around the snout and hold your mouth closed tight.

The success of the sock depends on how tight it fits. Most snouted werewolves will grow long enough to fill the sock so that its grip will keep the mouth clamped shut. It needs to fit tight enough that you can't tug it off. The sock can fail if you struggle too much during your change and shrug it out of place. In this case, you'll probably end up with your snout growing underneath the tube, and you'll quickly yank free of the sock once you're through your change. There have been no known cases of the sock asphyxiating a werewolf. It either works or gets tugged off immediately.

For short-snout werewolves, there is the muzzle halter suit.

The Muzzle Halter Suit

This is a one-piece neoprene and spandex head mask and partial-torso bodysuit. The head mask is designed much like the sort of masks you'll find at a fetish shop. Around the mouth and nose area is a panel of steel mesh that allows for airflow but stifles howling. The eyeholes allow for 100 percent visibility. The head mask extends down into a half-torso shirt with short sleeves for the arms. So the mask is held in place underneath the wolf's armpits.

Fetish Wear for Werewolves

There is already a thriving industry for the design and manufacture of restraints for humans. The field of S&M fetish-wear design is peopled with infinitely creative designers who have built careers and retail empires on the creation of astoundingly complex, practical restraint systems for adult men and women. Browsing S&M restraint designs can provide you with many ideas and, occasionally, the perfect template for what a werewolf needs.

You can't just buy off the rack, unfortunately. The customer for an S&M retailer is a non-lyc human. Therefore the product might be constructed of material that a wild werewolf could tear free of in an instant.

Not to worry. A fetish-wear designer worth his salt will be more than happy to work with the materials you request, provided the price is right. Such designers are always looking for new materials and new twists on construction. Don't worry about them getting suspicious about your use for the suit. These designers encounter all varieties of odd behavior, and any experienced designer will have learned long ago not to ask too many questions of their clients.

CHAPTER ELEVEN

Diet and Livestock

I've been a werewolf for damn near half a century now. When I change, I do it in a large, fenced-in area on a piece of property that's far from civilization. I've raised, attacked, and eaten just about anything that runs, flies, or wriggles. Sheep, pigs, cows, chickens, rabbits, alpacas, bison, goats, even ostrich—I've tried 'em all. I even ate skunks once. You heard me. I brought a colony of skunks inside the fence on the theory that they'd smell so goddamn bad, they'd keep curious folks away from my compound. I just figured I'd get used to the stench after a spell, and since I'd never remembered what the other animals I killed tasted like, why not eat skunk? Pretty smart, right? Wrong. It's been over forty years, and I sure as hell remember what skunk tastes like. Awful. I don't know that I'll ever forget it. Terrible. Just terrible.

—Jefferson H., Property Rights Lawyer (retired)

Age: 91, Lyc age: 48

WHY ARE WEREWOLVES SO HUNGRY?

Short of giving birth, the process of lycanthropic transformation is the most physically demanding task your body will ever perform. Over the course of a twenty-minute transformation, you could be gaining up to 150 pounds of additional muscle, bone, hair, flesh, and blood. This transformation requires every last ounce of stored energy you possess. When the change is complete, you will feel a need to replace that energy. The athletic killing machine that your body has turned into is impressive, and it needs refueling.

To satisfy this hunger and prevent yourself from getting loose, we recommend keeping either domesticated livestock or large quantities of raw meat on hand for every single Moon.

WOULDN'T IT BE SAFER TO JUST STARVE MYSELF DURING THE CHANGE?

Absolutely not.

Unlike a non-lyc, whose natural response to hunger is weakness, a werewolf in his wild state responds with adrenaline and rage. The hungrier you get, the more likely you are to break loose and hunt while transformed. Conversely, a werewolf with a full belly is happier, more docile, and far less likely to get loose. That is safer for you, your loved ones, and your community.

Additionally, if a werewolf does not feed during his Moons, the physical impact of that hunger is felt the next day, when the werewolf is back in his dormant state. If you have not eaten anything for several Moons, it would not be uncommon for you to awaken in your dormant form already suffering from advanced symptoms of starvation, including atrophying muscles, severe apathy, dehydration, body rashes, and in extreme cases, even heart failure.

WHAT SHOULD YOU EAT?

Fresh meat.

Werewolves prefer to hunt and feed on animal prey. Just after the change, you will hunt, attack, and devour the first human or animal you come across. If confined to a space where hunting is not an option, you will eat freshly slaughtered or raw meat, or even large bags of dog food.

HOW MUCH SHOULD YOU EAT?

While eating too little can be dangerous, eating too much can be expensive. In your wild state, you won't stop eating when you become full. You might overeat out of sheer boredom if trapped in a confined space. While there are few serious health risks associated with overeating in your wild state, it's dumb for you to pay for it. To address this, we recommend that you follow an easy "deal-a-meal" type chart (fig. 1) in order to make sure that you eat enough to sate your hunger, but not so much as to burn through your wallet unnecessarily.

A balanced meal

10-LB BAG OF
DOG FOOD: 10 PIPM
↓

Chow

SMALL LIVE
DONKEY: 95 LKP →

Our chart assigns different point values to various foodstuffs. The average werewolf will be completely sated once he has devoured enough food to provide a Point Intake Per Moon (PIPM) of 100 or more, providing that at least 40 of those points are gained by killing and devouring live prey. Werewolves are natural hunters, which is why, pound for pound, living prey is worth more PIPM. The energy expended in the killing of a live animal serves to calm you, whereas simply eating sacks or piles of stagnant meat or dog food will fuel your body, but won't quench your bloodlust. If you do not have access to 40 PIPM worth of living livestock on any given Moon, we recommend providing an additional 50 PIPM worth of food, bringing your total points per Moon to 150.

SHOULD I RAISE MY OWN ANIMALS FOR SLAUGHTER?

If you have the land to raise your own livestock for feeding during your Moons, by all means, go for it. There are books devoted to the subject of animal husbandry that go into far greater detail than we can here. Nonetheless, you are going to want to select animals that can live safely and discreetly in the area in which you plan to spend your Moons, and that will attract as little attention as possible, especially seeing as whatever it is you raise will be disappearing thrice a month.

WHAT KIND OF ANIMALS SHOULD I RAISE?

Werewolves have been accused of a great many things over the centuries, but never of being picky eaters. There are hundreds of different animals that you can choose from. While all of the standard domesticated farm animals that are appropriate for human consumption are more than adequate as food for hungry werewolves, we would like to pass on a few tips on the different varieties.

Large domesticated animals. The advantage to large domesticated animals is simple: leftovers. Cows are simply too big

FIGURE 1: WEREWOLF DEAL-A-MEAL CHART

Recommended Point Intake Per Moon (PIPM):

- 100 (if meal includes at least 40 Live Kill Points [LKP])
  - 150 (if food is either dead or motionless)

NOTE: This is a starting point only. We realize that werewolves, like people, come in all different shapes and sizes. These figures are based on an average Stage 1, twenty-eight-year-old, 180–pound male lycanthrope who transforms into a 330–pound werewolf. Adjust as necessary and, if in doubt, err on the side of more food.

10 pounds filler (must be mixed with at least 20 pounds ground meat) (slightly boiled potatoes, oatmeal, or tofu are ideal, as they absorb the flavor of the meat around them)	15 points
10-pound bag of dry dog food	10 points
20 pounds ground meat (either ground or chopped into manageable chunks)	40 points
Small live animal (10–15 pounds) (chicken, turkey, rabbit, cat, piglet, etc.)	30 points (LKP)
Medium-size live domesticated animal (75–135 pounds) (goat, lamb, small pig)	70 points (LKP)
Large live domesticated animal (80–200 pounds) (large pig or sheep, calf, small donkey, or mule)	95 points (LKP)
Extra-large live domesticated animal (200+ pounds) (cow, bison, oxen, alpaca, ostrich)	200 points (LKP)

a meal for you to completely devour over the course of a single eight-hour Moon. Therefore, on the evening of your first Moon, you can kill and partially devour, say, an ox and feed the remaining meat into a grinder on the following day. Then you'll eat the leftovers on your second and maybe third Moons, scoring them on the deal-a-meal chart as ground meat.

Not Recommended: Horses. While a werewolf is happy to kill and eat a horse, they are a nightmare to live with in your dormant state. Horses fear newly bitten lycanthropes, so much so that if you even walk past one, you can cause them to rear back and go wild. This can cause a terribly dangerous situation for you, not to mention the hassle of feeding and care. Additionally, most horses are prohibitively expensive. Stay away from them.

Small domesticated animals. While it might seem like small animals are not much of a meal for a werewolf, the fact is, it doesn't matter. Just eat a lot of them. If given the choice, you will almost always choose to hunt and kill a larger animal, but if there isn't that option, it's perfectly OK to eat smaller ones. Just make sure you have 100 PIPM worth, and you're all good.

YOU'RE BUSY THAT DAY

Come Thanksgiving 2015, better tell your folks to put dinner on early because you have to be someplace that night. Your second Moon of the month occurs on Thanksgiving night: Thursday, November 26, 2015. So you'd better fill up good and get a move on to your safe room. Take as many leftovers as you can carry. You'll definitely not be letting them go to waste that night.

Recommended: Rabbits. For those lycs who find themselves spending their Moons in relatively small quarters, you can't beat a dinner of a dozen or so live rabbits. While the downside is that you need a lot of them, you will find that their speed and agility require you to exert so much energy to catch each one, by the time you've eaten them all you're not only full, but you'll have had a decent bout of exercise and are ready to rest. Additionally, they reproduce so often and in such large numbers that with proper care and maintenance, a small investment in rabbits can sustain a hungry werewolf for a lifetime.

Not Recommended: Cats and Dogs. While domesticated cats and dogs are worth 10 easy PIPM each, provide a live kill, and are easily obtainable for no cost at local shelters, they are not recommended as food items. People just love them too much. Dogs and cats are beloved pets in households across the world, and local news crews like nothing more than a human-interest story about rescuing a dog or cat from a bad situation. Even if they never get wise about your lycanthropy, the news that pets are getting killed or even abused in any way could be enough for you to get locked up. Plus, cats hate werewolves, and you'll find it is a chore to have them around you. Unless you are very desperate, stay away from cats and dogs.

> **Famous Lycs Through Time**
> Minnie Pearl,
> Country Comedienne
> (1912–96, Lyc yrs: 1960–96)
> Her contract rider demanded recurring live rabbit deliveries to the set of *Hee Haw*.

Wild Animals/Game. While acquiring wild animals or game is not impossible (especially considering your enhanced sense of smell and hearing), it is difficult to keep them alive in captivity. Still, if you have a place to spend your Moons that is wide-open enough to allow wild animals (including yourself)

CAN A WEREWOLF BE A VEGETARIAN?

No. And if you were a vegetarian before you were bitten, we're sorry to report, that won't last long. A werewolf in his wild state will only eat vegetables and plants if they are mixed in with ground meat. A good way to cut costs is to have a large number of cooked potatoes, oatmeal, or tofu on hand, and blend them in with whatever raw meat you can find—the bloodier the better. While you'll ignore a bowl of plain potatoes when you're wild, if the spuds are cooked and stirred into ground meat at a ratio of two parts meat to one part filler, you will handily devour it when the time comes.

to roam relatively free, there is nothing quite like running down a deer or large moose, flying through the air for a magnificent kill, and feasting on the steaming meat. But we would like to stress that this is only recommended for those lycs who have the means to purchase their own compound, island, or plot of land, and to make sure that no humans will be stumbling across your path.

AFTER A WEREWOLF EATS, WHAT HAPPENS TO ALL THAT FOOD?

A werewolf's digestion, like many of its bodily functions, is tremendously accelerated. Anything that you eat, you will pass. Forty minutes or so before changing back to human form, a werewolf that has eaten well will generally have a large bowel movement. The day after a Moon, you will not have to eat all day and will likely have several large bowel movements as well. This is completely natural and nothing to be worried about, as your enhanced metabolism will process the food completely.

YOU'RE A WOLF-MAN, NOT A ROCKEFELLER: THERE IS NO REASON TO SPEND EXTRA MONEY ON HIGH-GRADE MEAT

According to the USDA, ground beef is assigned into eight categories or "grades." These are Prime, Choice, Select, Standard, Commercial, Utility, Cutter, and Canner. The lowest grades, Utility, Cutter, and Canner, are all perfectly edible and primarily used for canned food and hot dogs. In your wild state, you will never know the difference, and even if it is slightly tainted, your heightened immune system will easily be able to digest just about anything short of pure poison. These low grades of beef are rarely sold in stores, but can easily be obtained directly from slaughterhouses.

We also recommend purchasing an industrial-size meat grinder. Any bones or leftover flesh that remain the morning after a Moon can be fed into the grinder along with your filler, creating a raw, ground-meat mixture that can be devoured later in the Moon Set or frozen and saved for the future.

Werewolf Wanted

I was really flying high, man. Making more money than my parents, and I wasn't even out of high school! The sky was the limit. But then I got bit. My first Moon, we were nearing the end of a shoot, and I just disappeared for three days. They found me in the desert. I couldn't tell anyone I was a werewolf, so when they started talking like it was drugs I let 'em. Well, that made it so I couldn't be insured for any more movies, so I stopped getting work. Then I started with the drugs for real. Tried using a lotta pills to keep my Moons in check, but I just ended up getting addicted. Now I'm pushing forty and I have all my hopes pinned on this miserable reality show.

—Name withheld, former child actor

Age: 38, Lyc age: 22

SO I GUESS I CAN'T WORK NOW THAT I'M A WEREWOLF, RIGHT?

Sorry, deadbeat. Not only can lycanthropes work, but you are going to need to find yourself a good source of cash pretty quick. As it happens, being a werewolf is expensive. You know how they say owning a boat is like standing in the shower and ripping up one-hundred-dollar bills? Same thing goes for lycanthropy (except the drain's clogged with fur).

It'd be nice if werewolves only bit the independently wealthy, but sadly, their palates are not quite so refined. As a werewolf, you need to spend money on a safe room, maybe restraints, and meat or livestock to feed on during your Moons, just to name a few necessities. Financially, it's not all that different from having a baby (but you don't get to claim your beastly alter ego as a dependent). With one turn of events, all of your carefree days are over, and you suddenly start bleeding money into a single expense. Except instead of nurturing a life, you're preventing yourself from taking life.

A JOB FIT FOR A WEREWOLF

Employment is one of the more pressing concerns in the very turbulent life of the Stage 1 lycanthrope. It is very often the case that a new lycanthrope has to change his employment situation to fit his new lifestyle. Your financial demands as well as scheduling concerns can force you to switch careers or give up on less practical pursuits, such as the arts or social work, which might not pay as well.

What Should a Lycanthrope Look For in a Job?

The following are conditions of employment that a lycanthrope needs to pursue:

Good pay. To cover the expenses of securing yourself and satisfying your appetite during your Moons.

Flexible schedule. You need those three nights out of the month off. And it would be really handy to have the mornings after free as well, since you might not wake up from your Moons ready to put your nose to the grindstone (especially if you get loose, God forbid).

No drug testing or physical examination. You can't have your fluids analyzed. They will detect irregularities. To avoid detection, never give blood or urine to a physician or lab technician for analysis.

No security clearances/background checks. Avoid high-profile work in government or public office that requires extensive background checks for security clearance. Also, avoid positions in financial institutions that require a release of your financial records and credit history. A close look at your finances might reveal a trail of odd purchases (restraints, cage-

---

JOB INTERVIEW TIPS FOR WEREWOLVES

Here are some tips to help lycanthropes nail that job interview:

- **Be enthusiastic.** It doesn't matter if you're only pursuing this new job because it fits your lifestyle. You have to make your interviewer think you've been working toward this job your whole life.
- **Be ready to explain your schedule.** Make up a story about a sick relative that needs to be taken to a physician on a regular basis or a story about a child custody situation, something that an employer won't think is negotiable. The time off you need each month is not too much to ask (leaving work early on your Moons, maybe coming in late on post-Moon mornings), but you do need a good story to explain it.
- **Be careful not to interview near a Moon day.** If your Moon is approaching, you won't be able to help but seem edgy, perhaps even a little hostile. Same as if you just had a Moon. You might be worn out and could have trouble making it to the appointment if you get loose or have trouble getting out of your restraints. Have a day or two cushion around your Moons when scheduling your interview.
- **Whatever you do, don't be yourself.** Being yourself might be the best policy for a non-lyc, but as a lycanthrope, you're trying to hide a key element of your existence. Lies and evasiveness are the way to go.

building materials, livestock) that will draw unwanted attention.

Werewolves don't need health insurance! Unless you have a family to care for, you no longer need to be concerned about whether a job provides good health benefits. You want to stay away from doctors from now on, so as to avoid anyone getting a good look at your biological makeup, and your body's regenerative powers will make most medical treatment unnecessary. So you can pursue more freelance or under-the-table work that you might have ignored before because they didn't provide the health benefits that are so necessary to non-lyc human life.

The Werewolf Career Counselor Is In

What kind of jobs should a lycanthrope pursue? There are numerous jobs for which lycanthropes are suitable, though you might not have considered them before you were bitten. This list should be seen as a resource for those seeking immediate employment with good pay and will not include careers that would require substantial training or schooling (law, medicine, etc.):

Waiter/waitress. It's easy to get and can pay well if you work at the right restaurant, and your income is hard to document come tax time. Your increased strength and stamina will keep you from tiring out too quickly. You'll be working nights, but the waiter's schedule is extremely flexible, and it is not hard to request your Moon nights off. In fact, if you're only requesting three nights off per month, you might be considered the lowest-maintenance server on staff.

Office temp. Easy to get if you have basic typing and computer skills. Can pay very well since you're not getting benefits. Best of all, the schedule is completely up to you. Be careful of dry spells, though. At less-busy times of year (summer, around the holidays) temps are less in demand, which means less work for you.

Professional mover. You are now capable of sprinting while holding a couch. Movers usually get paid under the table, and they're always in demand.

Lumberjack. More of a regional job, of course. But your physical prowess now more than qualifies you for this sort of rugged work.

Bounty hunter/bail bondsman. How better to turn lemons into lemonade than to use your physical superiority to put criminals behind bars? You work on your own schedule, and the money is very good. And your enhanced sensory sensitiv-

---

DON'T BELIEVE IT!
WEREWOLF ASSASSIN SQUADS

There is no such thing as a covert team of lycanthropes who are paid to infiltrate targeted regimes or organizations with the intent of purposely loosing themselves during their Moons on whoever is targeted for assassination. While the werewolf is a killing machine, it is not a very efficient one. Werewolves cannot be trained to kill a target. They hunt prey based on instinct and hunger. A werewolf assassin could fail in his assassination if he simply comes upon another person to eat before reaching his target. It's silly to think that such an organization could ever exist. So if you've recently been bitten and are looking for work, don't expect any operatives to come knocking on your door asking if you'd like to join their squad.

ity and hunting skills are a huge asset. The only drawback is that you'll be in direct contact with the police. You always want to be careful to avoid drawing the attention of law enforcement, even if you're working with them. (See Chapter 19, "Government and Police.")

Bouncer/doorman. As long as you can request nights off for your Moons, no problem.

Bodyguard. Employment as an escort with a security firm is a possibility. You'd be sent out on short-term assignments, and you would have some schedule flexibility. But you might run into difficulty if you contracted with a single individual and started requesting certain nights off every month. Note that some firms require that their security escorts be bonded.

Any union trade labor. Unless you are already in a union or you know someone who can get you in, this isn't very practical. But if this work is available to you, it pays very well and has lots of scheduling freedom.

Package delivery. Delivery carriers with Federal Express or UPS can make good money, and there are various schedule options due to the many shifts required. Again, your brawn will keep you from burning out too soon.

---------- **TRUE LEGENDS?** ----------

WEREWOLVES AS PETS FOR WEALTHY ECCENTRICS?
YOU BET!

The extremely wealthy occasionally run out of cool things to buy, so some of them have started hunting down the stuff of legend just to add a rare and hard-to-attain item to their assets column. There have been several lycanthropes who have been acquired by the wealthy as pets, and it's apparently a pretty sweet gig. The lycanthropes are usually given the most attentive and lavish care, everything from two-story fortified cages to the finest livestock for feeding. All the lycanthrope has to do in turn is consent to being treated like a freak to being gawked at by the rich. The pet owner will occasionally throw parties on the night of the lyc's Moon and keep the lycanthrope in a cage in the middle of the festivities so that everyone can gather around and watch the beast struggle against his captivity or feed on livestock.

Of course, there have been incidents where the wealthy eccentric wanted to go even further and explore the lycanthrope sexually. Remember, your instincts are extremely sharp. Trust them. If the situation feels creepy, it probably is.

CHAPTER THIRTEEN

Romance and the Modern Lycanthrope

After he got bitten, it took a while before we were comfortable with sex again. We just weren't sure what the risks were. The risks to me. He went away for the first few months. I guess he wanted to keep me safe.

Once we were man and wife again, believe it or not, it kind of helped us out. I always loved him, but there was something a little bit missing in the bedroom. That kind of abandon you can only experience when you're with someone you have no intention of making a life with, but someone you only want to make the next fifteen minutes with. I had just assumed that when you find the one you love, the sex is more tender. And more tame.

Since he got bitten . . . a lot of words come to mind. Tame isn't one of them.

—Linda P., Journalist and Wife of a Lycanthrope
Age: 38, Non-lycanthrope

DO LOVE AND LYCANTHROPY MIX?

If you're single and you just got bitten by a werewolf, whether or not you can continue to date is probably not the foremost question in your mind. But if you're married or in a committed relationship, you're probably worried about your partner, your family, and the danger you now pose to them.

This chapter will focus on lycanthrope relationships and how you can continue to enjoy the fruits of a marriage, a family, or a committed partnership even though you're now a werewolf. To avoid redundancy, it will be assumed that whether you live with a roommate, a lover, or a spouse and children, you are taking the necessary precautions to ensure that no harm comes to them during your Moons. This chapter will only address questions specific to your romantic options and the possibility for a committed relationship with a werewolf.

CAN A WEREWOLF MAINTAIN A MARRIAGE?

With more than 50 percent of marriages ending in divorce, keeping a marriage or relationship from falling apart is hard enough without the added headache of one partner transmogrifying into a three-hundred-pound bloodthirsty predator three times a month. But marriages can survive all types of problems and even grow stronger for them. Consider the married couple that stays together after the death of a child, or a spouse's recovery from substance abuse, or an infidelity. All sorts of upheavals test the marital bond, but a strong marriage can still triumph. Dealing with one partner's lycanthropy should be no different.

There is one way for a lycanthrope's marriage to a non-lyc to remain safe, healthy, and thriving, and that's honesty. Unfortunately, lycanthrope honesty is difficult to reconcile with the whole "lie to everyone about your condition at all costs" situation. As always, we counsel secrecy above all else, but when it comes to your loved ones we realize that secrecy can be fatal. If your spouse doesn't know the dangers posed by your condition, all of your precautions could amount to nothing. Unless you're ready to leave him or her, you'll have to share your secret.

DON'T JUST RUN AND HIDE

It may be tempting to conceal your condition and simply establish a safe room far away from your home, keeping your family safe from an attack and safe from having to deal with what you've become. But lying to your spouse and disappearing on a regular basis will invariably arouse suspicion. If you appear to be hiding something, your spouse may try to follow you in secret. Everything will be going fine until the one month when you'll be holed up in your safe room, and your spouse storms in expecting to find you in bed with somebody, but instead finds you've turned into a flesh-hungry beast eager to tear into your spouse's rib cage and feed. All of your painstaking preparation will be undone by the simple fact that you failed to be honest.

WHAT IF I DON'T TRUST/DON'T LIKE MY SPOUSE?

If your marriage is already on the rocks, throwing your lycanthropy into the mix is not going to help turn you two around. You should probably see your werewolf attack as that final kick in the pants to dissolve the relationship and move on with your life. It takes a lot of love for a couple to deal with one partner's lycanthropy, and if that love isn't there, it's just not going to work out. Most importantly, if the trust isn't there, you run the risk of your spouse exposing you after the marriage inevitably disintegrates. Explore your feelings. If it's over, call it quits now.

WEREWOLF BOYFRIENDS AND WEREWOLF GIRLFRIENDS

If you are in an unmarried, committed relationship, your lycanthropy will likely force you to take that relationship to the next step, whether that be marriage, an even deeper commitment, or a breakup. Before you got bitten, you might have thought you had all the time in the world to figure your feelings out. Now that you've been bitten, lives are at stake. It's time to decide where this relationship is going and whether this is really "the one" who won't flip out and try to have you committed when you try to convince him or her that you're a werewolf.

HAVING "THE TALK"

Lay it all out on the table

Your partner must be made aware of the grave danger posed by coming into contact with you during your Moon. Make clear the precautions you must take and the rules that must

YOU'RE BUSY THAT DAY

Get ready to disappoint someone special on Valentine's Day 2014. That year, your second Moon of the month falls on February 14. Which means instead of sitting down to an overpriced prix fixe meal for two, you'll be chained up in your basement getting ready to gorge on a pile of dead flesh. We're aware that a good many of you might not see this as a bad thing.

be followed in order to ensure your partner's safety. You must also be open about the costs of these precautions and in what ways you and your partner will have to rebudget your expenses. If you have had to switch jobs or are planning to do so, state that plainly. Keep nothing to yourself and there will be no surprises down the line. Remember, even the smallest secret can put your partner in peril. If you are not being honest, you are doing your partner harm.

Be Convincing

The hardest part of having the talk is getting your partner to believe you. It is perfectly natural for your partner to be incredulous, and possibly to question your sanity. You probably didn't even believe in werewolves until not long after you got bitten by one. Your partner will need convincing, and you should not take his or her disbelief as an affront to the trust the two of you share.

Go to the Video

Seeing is believing. Unfortunately, if your partner were actually to be in the room with you in your wild state, it would be his or her end. A video of your transformation, however, can provide the evidence that your partner needs to be convinced. Install a camera in your safe room, someplace up high where

BREAKING THE ICE

You might find the hardest part of having the talk is figuring out where to start. Here are some sample first lines to break the ice on this very touchy conversation:

1. You know how all my hair grew back? It wasn't the Rogaine.

2. Remember when you confessed that you only floss when you know you have a dentist appointment coming up? Well, I have a confession too.

3. I have six months to live. Kidding! I'm just a werewolf.

4. You know how I said that I volunteered to be a Cub Scout troop leader even though we don't have any kids, and every month I have to take the troop on a three-day camping trip? Well, that wasn't entirely the truth.

5. I have good news and bad news. The good news is I'm not a vampire.

---

it won't be damaged during your change but with a clear enough sightline that there can be no question of the veracity of the recording.

Important: Destroy or delete the video immediately after viewing. Should video footage of a werewolf transformation fall into the wrong hands, it could be very dangerous for you, and possibly for all werewolves, if that tape were disseminated and a panic ensued.

Be Patient

Your partner will need some time to come to terms with what you've become, and it's quite possible that he or she will not be able to live with your new incarnation. The best you can do is try to make it clear to your partner that you are still the same person you've always been, full of the same love for your partner that you've always had. Though your physical form might change three times a month, your heart is still the same.

Howlanon

After you lay it all on the table, your partner might feel a bit overwhelmed. Lycanthropy is a lot to deal with, and a partner with lycanthropy is no picnic. There is a group specifically for the spouses and loved ones of werewolves. It's called Howlanon, and it's an organization for people who have a lycanthrope loved one in their lives, where they can share the trials and turmoil of standing by their werewolves, no matter how weird things might get. Information about the group can be found online at *howlanon.org*.

There Is Such a Thing As Being Too Close

To many people, being in a committed relationship means sharing everything, no matter how great the burden. In some instances, your partner might feel terrible that you have to go through this alone. The idea might come up that with a single bite from you in your wild state, you and your partner could share this ordeal together.

This is a form of fur chasing. (For more on this see Chapter 21, "Fur Chasers.") It should be obvious what a monumental error it would be to pursue this line of thinking. When you're a new lycanthrope still struggling to accept your fate and you feel entirely isolated from the rest of the human race, if the person you love the most says he or she is willing to go through it with you, it can be very tempting.

Don't do it. Don't even think about it, and under no circumstances should you entertain the conversation for even a second. You have to remember, and remind your partner, that a werewolf does not hunt people to try and make other werewolves. A werewolf wants only to feed. To kill. And it will stop at nothing to murder its prey. It's rare that someone manages to suffer a werewolf attack and survive. The possibility of an untrained non-lyc intentionally confronting a werewolf during a Moon and surviving is so unlikely it would be miraculous.

It is important to make it clear to your partner that this suggestion is absolutely preposterous. If you appear to entertain the idea at all, your partner might think you're refusing only because you can't bring yourself to put him or her in harm's way, and so your partner might take it upon him- or herself to simply show up at your safe room during your Moon and get bitten without your consent. Be firm. Under no circumstances should you allow for any discussion of this at all.

Be Open and Let Your Partner Help

The best way to keep your partner from wanting to be a werewolf is to make sure he or she is as involved in managing your lycanthropy as possible. Include your partner in decisions about your safe room location or feeding ideas. Bring your partner with you shopping for restraints and hardware. Share all of your concerns and fears with your partner, and he or she will never feel left out of your new life.

Relish the Time You Have Together

Many couples faced with lycanthropy discover a newfound closeness and tenderness together. In light of the dangers that you must face, your time together is no longer something to be taken for granted. The small problems you used to argue and obsess over can suddenly disappear, and if you let it, every day together can feel like a gift.

WEREWOLF SEX

Can Werewolves Have Sex?

Lycanthropes can rarely have sex while wild. During your Moons, you'll really only want to hunt. If by some chance during one of your Moons you happen upon a werewolf of the opposite sex, there is a remote possibility that you could have sex with that werewolf. But this would require that you both have already eaten to satisfaction, and that you meet in an area where you are both comfortably certain that there is no danger. It's very unlikely, but it happens.

As to the rest of the month: yes, you can have sex. When dormant, you will react to stimuli in much the same way you always have. This includes erotic triggers that stimulate arousal. The one major difference: your experience of sex is magnificently enhanced, thanks to the enhancement of your sensory perception of the physical world. Some have compared the lycanthrope's sexual pleasure to that of a human who has taken the drug MDMA, or Ecstasy. The pleasure derived from activity more commonly associated with foreplay will be experienced with an intensity that rivals most non-lyc orgasms.

Lycanthrope Orgasms

When it comes to the climax itself, most accounts of the experience equate it to a kind of fever dream, and many claim to have lost consciousness altogether, unsure afterward of which sensations were real and which were dreamed. There have been reports of lycanthropes suffering brief bouts of dementia immediately following orgasm, but despite the apparently explosive nervous activity involved, there have been no recorded instances of a lycanthrope orgasm causing any lasting brain damage.

Get Ready for a Wild Ride

The animal component of the lycanthrope's nature also affects the lycanthrope's sexual pursuit in ways that seem a little more, well, savage. This is not to say that you now pose a sexual assault threat. But in many cases, you will pursue a sexual partner with increased immediacy, and thanks to your sudden spike in virility, that pursuit is often successful.

Should Werewolves Have Sex?

Is sex with a lycanthrope safe? There are many worries about what can be communicated via intercourse with a lycanthrope, so we will address each individually.

Is Lycanthropy Sexually Communicable?

No. A person can become a lycanthrope only by being bitten by a werewolf during a Moon or being born of a lycanthrope father. (For more on werewolf babies, refer to Chapter 4, "Purebloods.") If a lycanthrope bites you or if you exchange fluids with a lycanthrope outside of his Moon, you will not become a lycanthrope.

Are Lycanthropes Still Vulnerable to Common Human STDs Such As AIDS?

Yes. Even though you have a different biological makeup, you can still catch HIV and other sexually transmitted diseases from unprotected sex.

Thanks to your regenerative powers, however, lycanthropes are less likely to be carriers of sexually transmitted disease. But remember, "less likely" should not imply a 0 percent risk of STDs. Regeneration of cells requires time, and if one sleeps with a lycanthrope immediately after the lycanthrope has contracted an STD, it is possible that the infection will still be active and communicable. Condoms are still the safest bet to avoid STDs.

TRUE LEGENDS?

"I HAVE TO GO AWAY AGAIN THIS MONTH"

Once upon a time, a man met a woman and they hit it off. They began dating, and it wasn't long before they were inseparable, save for a couple of days every month, right around the full moon. For the man was a lycanthrope, and he was not yet ready to tell his new love about his condition for fear of scaring her away. So he made excuses and disappeared for his Moons.

What surprised the man was how easily his excuses were accepted. Oftentimes he didn't even have to make an excuse since the woman would already have plans to be away for some trip or previous engagement. After his Moons, the man was never questioned about whatever trip he'd lied about. The woman seemed to have no curiosity about why he had to be unavailable on such a regular basis.

This made the man curious, and suspicious. He wondered if the woman was having an affair. He knew he couldn't confront her without confessing to the lies he'd told and why he'd told them. But his suspicions nagged at him enough that he finally decided it was worth the risk of scaring her off in order to clear the air.

He sat her down at her kitchen table and told her everything. He told her what he was doing all those times he had to be away. He did his best to reassure her that he was taking the precautions to keep her safe. Then he asked her, "Now that you know what I am, and what I've been doing every month, is there anything you'd like to tell me?"

She said nothing. Instead, she took his hand and led him from the kitchen down to her basement, where she unlocked a thick steel door to reveal an air-tight, soundproof chamber with an elaborate restraint system dangling from her ceiling.

"And here's what I've been doing every month," she said with a smile.

Then they kissed, he proposed, and the lycanthrope couple started making plans to move to a house big enough for his-and-hers safe rooms.

(This oft-told story may not be true. It's hard to believe that the two lycanthropes would not be able to smell each other. But it's romantic enough and just possible enough that we're going to choose to believe.)

CHAPTER FOURTEEN

Werewolf Communities

You'd think that a bunch of werewolves living together would be done in by something sinister. But our little experiment was done in by the weather. A hurricane hit on a Moon night. It was supposed to just graze us, but it came down way worse than predicted. We were all chained and restrained when our basements started flooding. Most drowned. Some were buried alive under debris. Only a few of us made it out alive. But boy I bet the Red Cross was freaked out when they found so many victims chained up like that. The survivors got away before we could be questioned. I'll never try to live with a bunch of lycs again. It's too damn dangerous.

—Coleman B., Convenience Store Franchise Rep

Age: 41, Lyc age: 19

BELIEVE IT OR NOT, IT'S HARD FOR A WHOLE GROUP OF PEOPLE TO CUT THEMSELVES OFF FROM THE REST OF SOCIETY IN THIS DAY AND AGE

It was much easier to form a lycanthrope community before the population explosion started filling up the globe with people, and before the technological advancements that make it so easy to keep track of them all. In modern America, when a group of people try to set up a community outside of the rest of society, they're called separatists, and they usually don't exist for too long before being surrounded by ATF agents.

Unless you're hiding up in the Appalachian hills or on some empty swath of land in Montana, you really can't just wall yourself off from the rest of society. Eventually, someone's going to come nosing around demanding you pay taxes or sign a petition.

Several known lycanthrope-established and occupied communities have existed throughout the world at different points in time. Whether any such communities are currently in existence we prefer not to say. It is possible to establish a lycanthrope community, if very difficult. What makes it so hard?

It's just not practical

WHY LYCANTHROPE COMMUNITIES ARE A BAD IDEA

It's Supposed to Be a Secret

Joining a lycanthrope community means outing yourself to other lycanthropes, which puts your life at risk. As stated in Chapter 18, "Avoiding Detection," the minute you tell someone about your condition—even another lycanthrope—your life is in danger.

This isn't like the gay community, where you embrace

your identity and force the world to accept you as you really are. Even if you were to form a community of fifty lycanthropes living in harmony, instead of just one lycanthrope trying to keep his lycanthropy a secret, you'd be fifty lycanthropes all at once trying to keep one gigantic, furry secret. Someone's gonna talk.

You Should Trust a Werewolf About As Far As You Can Throw Him

It is very dangerous to think that you can trust another lycanthrope simply because you're both in the same boat. There is no reason to assume that a werewolf wants to be within a hundred miles of another werewolf. How does he know if you're being diligent with your restraints? If you get loose, the townspeople could come hunting *him* down. Oh, and by the way, werewolves are dangerous! Just because you happen to be one doesn't mean you want to be in the vicinity of another one.

Hunting in Packs Is Not a Great Idea

When lycs dream of a werewolf community, they often envision a pack of werewolves out hunting together, roaming the lands and protecting each other from dangers.

A werewolf pack is technically possible, but highly impractical and very dangerous. First, if your community does not reside far from a populated area, you should not be loose on your Moon, no matter how many of you there are. Second, unless wolves are born into their pack, the hierarchy is formed through aggression and violence, which means you and your werewolf buddies will have to fight it out to decide the alpha werewolf in charge of the pack. This can result in, of course, death, or at least dismemberment. You might wake up from your Moon missing a finger or an eyeball.

Three Nights Out of the Month, Your Community Would Be Helpless

Unless you have somehow found a magical swath of land where you are all able to roam free on your Moons, everyone in your community will probably have to lock themselves away for their change. Which means that one thousand lycanthropes living together in a community is still a community that is completely defenseless three nights out of every month. That's thirty-six nights a year, more than an entire month, when your entire society is nothing but a bunch of werewolves chained up in their homes, vulnerable to whatever might befall your town. What if there's a fire? Or a flood? Or what if a werewolf hunter discovered your little oasis and knew damn well that if he showed up on a full moon he'd be able to burn down the whole town without a single person standing in his way?

Famous Lycs Through Time

Norman Rockwell,
Painter/Illustrator
(1894–1978, Lyc yrs: 1940–78)
In later life, embarked on a series of works entitled *The American Large Intestine*, which depicted various small-town Americans in idyllic settings with their bellies torn open. These works are believed to have been lost in a studio fire.

In light of this, guess who's really handy to have around your werewolf community? People who aren't werewolves! That's right, the safest lycanthrope community is one that is not *all lycanthropes*. You need at least a few non-lyc citizens to be on the ball while you all are "indisposed." These will likely be spouses and blood relatives of lycanthropes, loved ones who are willing to accept the duty of looking after a town full of flesh-hungry beasts three times a month.

WOLF MEETUPS

A modern day lycanthrope community is more likely one that is less about a bunch of werewolves living next door to one another and more about werewolves who are acquainted with one another and maintain some form of contact, whether it be in person or electronically.

In the post-WWII era, before the Internet age, lycanthrope social interaction usually occurred in public places such as bars and coffeehouses. These gatherings were called "Howlers," and they were far more frequent in cities than anywhere else. Howlers occurred midmonth, as far from a full moon as possible, and they were casual social gatherings in which lycs could be around other lycs for nothing more than camaraderie. It was understood that you didn't speak openly about your lycanthropy, or anything that could draw suspicion upon your group from eavesdroppers. If information needed to be shared, such as news of a lyc hunter's arrival in town or an investigation following a loose wolf, it was done after the Howler, one lyc to another, and the information was passed on in a similar fashion. One mouth to one ear. Never to the group.

Howlers are less frequent now, and less necessary. Internet werewolf communities have taken their place. Werewolves stay connected via coded websites or password-protected message boards. These sites allow lycanthropes to maintain anonymity while still reaching out to others like them. Internet communities can help lycanthropes share information and advice and can alleviate the loneliness many lycanthropes experience. We won't publish these sites' URLs to maintain their privacy, but you can find them via an Internet search for werewolf communities. There are many dummy sites and role-playing sites out there, and you'll know the fakes immediately by the false information contained therein. When you find a real online werewolf community, you'll probably be confronted with some questions before being granted access. They'll be questions only a werewolf can answer correctly.

HOW TO INTRODUCE YOURSELF TO ANOTHER LYCANTHROPE

Again, you know our recommendation: *don't*. That said, being a werewolf can make you feel more alone than you ever thought possible. If you feel it's absolutely crucial to meet another lyc, here are our suggestions.

Anonymity. Remaining anonymous is essential for the initial contact. If you've identified a lycanthrope by scent, you can't just walk right up to him and introduce yourself. He'll probably pretend not to know what you're talking about (if he's not stupid). The best way to go about it is to slip the lycanthrope an anonymous note. If you spot him at dinner or at a bar, drop the note in his coat pocket when he gets up to go to the bathroom. The note should not make it obvious that you're both werewolves should someone else find it. But it should be obvious to the lycanthrope. Mention something only a werewolf would understand. Talk about fingernail clipping or odor masking. Ask him when he was bitten. Just don't leave a name or a way to contact you. The purpose of the note is just to let the other lyc know that you're on to him and to get him prepared for when you finally do choose to reveal yourself.

You eventually have to tell the lycanthrope how he can contact you. It's recommended that you not do so in the first note. The lycanthrope has every reason to think you're a werewolf hunter trying to get him to identify himself. It's best

Discretion is essential

to wait until a Moon has passed since your first contact before you invite the lycanthrope to contact you. If you were a werewolf hunter watching him, you would have been watching during his Moon and you would have no reason to wait to kill him. After the Moon has passed, give the lycanthrope a designated public place where he can leave you a message. Perhaps he can leave you a letter under a rock in a park. Or you can ask him to scratch the word "fang" into the wall of a public bathroom stall if he wishes that the two of you meet in person.

The most important thing about anonymity is that a trust begins to develop before either of you is exposed to each other. After you've relinquished your anonymity and the two of you meet, you're on your own.

TRUE LEGENDS?

LYCANTHROPES USED TO COMMUNICATE WITH ONE ANOTHER VIA KOZMO.COM

In the 1990s several online delivery services enjoyed a brief popularity before foundering after failing to turn a profit that would justify their investment capital. Kozmo.com was one of the more popular sites, and there were several others that emulated Kozmo's model of immediate (within an hour) delivery of retail items selected online, such as DVD rentals, CDs, and snacks like ice cream and Starbucks coffee.

Lycanthropes began using these sites as an anonymous messenger service. If one lycanthrope discovered the arrival of a lyc hunter in an area, he would go online to Kozmo.com and order a predetermined movie title (usually *Forrest Gump* or a similarly huge hit that was likely to be overstocked and would not raise any eyebrows when a lot of copies went out at once) to be delivered to as many lycanthropes as he knew lived in that area. The DVD would arrive at the lycanthropes' homes, alerting them to the news and warning them to prepare for an attack. Those lycs who received the movie would have their own list of lycs to send a copy to, and they'd go online and continue the Kozmo.com chain letter.

Lycanthropes communicated anonymously in this manner until the sites began their decline. By 2000, when it became apparent that werewolves were the only people still using these online delivery services, it was decided that the services were too dangerous to be used for communication, and werewolves were forced to look for other ways to share information.

CHAPTER FIFTEEN

Of God, the Devil, and Lycanthrope Faith

No, I don't believe in God, and if he exists, he should be glad I don't believe in him. If I did, I'd be sending a whole lot of pissed-off prayers his way demanding to know why he created some men in a way that they should be forced to spend three nights of every month chained up in a basement. Real smart, God. Were you high that day, or what?

—Stevie G., Telemarketer

Age: 26, Lyc age: 10

MUST I TURN MY BACK ON GOD NOW THAT I'M A WEREWOLF?

Though your body has changed, there is no reason to assume your soul has too. Your lycanthropy should not prevent you from continuing to embrace your faith with the same passion you've always had. Your new struggles might test your faith, but no more so than the woman stricken with cancer or a debilitating handicap who begins to question the wisdom or existence of God.

Though you might be able to hang on to your faith, you will be far less capable of obeying your religion's moral code. It is very likely, for example, that you will take the life of a human being, perhaps several, and you'll have to make peace with your God somehow. Rather than break with God at these times, many lycanthropes have said that their faith in God is what keeps them going and gives them the strength to live a safer life and avoid harming others.

DON'T CONFESS

Confessing sins to a clergy member, a tenant of Catholicism and orthodox Christianity, is one sacrament lycanthropes will have to forgo. Remember, your condition is a secret. If you've gotten loose and you've killed, your confessor will demand that you atone for your sins by owning up to the crime. Since imprisonment for you means guaranteed death or worse, you must skip confession and find your own atonement elsewhere.

WEREWOLVES CAN'T KEEP KOSHER
(YOU CAN FORGET ABOUT OTHER DIETARY RESTRICTIONS TOO)

If your religion has any dietary restrictions in regards to the consumption of meat, you'd better start getting accustomed to a life of sin. There is, to our knowledge, no religion with dietary restrictions that makes allowances for the possibility that some in their congregation might have no choice but to feed on raw flesh three nights out of every month.

ARE YOU A CREATION OF THE DEVIL?

Not that we know of.

Throughout history, werewolves have been accused of being the spawn of Satan, especially by those attempting to justify the necessity of exterminating the lycanthrope race. Werewolves have been accused of being soldiers of the devil, acting under Satan's command to wreak bloody havoc on earth. Some folklore has said that a werewolf can only be born from a human being's voluntary pact with the devil, while other tales propose that lycanthropy manifests only as the result of a curse cast upon a human being's soul.

The assumption that werewolves must have some satanic or occult heritage can be attributed to there being almost no documented medical research into the biological agents of lycanthropy. The existence of the hormone lycantropin in the human body proves that lycanthropy is an innately human condition. Unfortunately, almost all research into lycanthropy has either been suppressed by the medical community or conducted in secrecy by government scientists. Without trusted scientific documentation, simple minds have no choice but to turn to occult forces to make sense of what they cannot understand. If more people could see that the forces behind a werewolf's change are the work of a bodily hormone that we all possess, they might feel less of a need to rely on black magic for an explanation.

Some werewolves, after having gotten loose and making a kill, might embrace these explanations in order to cope with the massive guilt they're now forced to shoulder. It would be much easier to accept having committed as monstrous an act as murder if you were simply doing the bidding of God or Satan. Religious fanaticism is a dangerous fallback for the lycanthrope, as it's a step toward relinquishing control and responsibility for his own actions. (For more on this, see Chapter 23, "The Dark Side of Lycanthropy.")

CHAPTER SIXTEEN

Health, Medicine, and Wellness

There are definitely some things you can avoid if you want to stay healthy—"people with machine guns" springs to mind. But if you keep your nose clean and live by your calendar, your physical health should work itself out. And know who you are. "God, grant me the serenity to accept the things I cannot change, the courage to change the things I can, and the wisdom to know the difference." I learned that back in AA. It works pretty good for lycanthropy, too. Oh, and it can't hurt to get a flu shot every once in a while, you know, if they're handin' 'em out at work. Just to keep up appearances.

—Doug C., Parish Sexton
Age: 59, Lyc age: 30

PART ONE: HEALTHY BODY

From the moment the lycantropin hormone is activated in your body, you will rarely get sick, almost never get serious illnesses, and will be practically immune to the kinds of nagging physical aches and pains that those people not living with lycanthropy are forced to deal with as their bodies slowly wear out with age. The reason for this, of course, is that your body, unlike the vast majority of the population, naturally regenerates itself three times a month. Lycanthropy affects the human body like a powerful steroid. Cells, bones, muscle, and organs are broken down and regrown—in most cases leaving them stronger than before.

Healing Faster, Living Longer

The transformation process involves the breakdown and re-building of much of the body's muscle and tissue. This process mends any creeping infirmities that might cause long-term damage otherwise. So if you are wounded or battered in your wild state, by the time you transform back to your dormant state your wounds will be well on the way to being healed, with all evidence of the wounds likely to have disappeared within a few days' time.

Accelerated healing doesn't only occur during your Moon, however. While the transformation process comes to a head around the full moon, the process is ongoing at a less notice-able rate throughout the month. All month long, lycantropin acts upon your organs and tissues, steadily causing cells to be broken down and regenerated. A simple cut suffered in your dormant state will rarely take longer than twenty-four hours to close up.

So I'm Immortal?

You might heal more quickly, but you aren't indestructible. If you get stabbed, that wound will heal very quickly, since the ingredients are already there for the tissue harmed in that wound to be rebuilt. But if your arm gets cut off at the shoul-der, it's not going to grow back simply because you're a were-wolf. The transformation process breaks down and rebuilds the structures of your body. If there's no arm to break down, it's not getting rebuilt.

Whether in your dormant or wild state, you still require a working heart pumping blood to the brain and throughout your body. Getting your head blown off, taking a gunshot to the heart, or suffering massive blood loss will still likely lead to your death, which is why so much of this book deals with the precautions werewolves must take in order to avoid physical danger.

Lycanthropy Can't Produce Miracles

Some people hear of the lycanthrope's capacity for healing, and they immediately assume that getting bitten by a werewolf is a magical cure-all. There have even been instances when terminally ill patients have sought out lycanthrope blood in the hopes that becoming a werewolf will rid them of their ailments.

While lycanthropes can heal much more quickly and successfully than non-lycs, it's important to note that the regeneration in the lycanthrope body can only work with what is already there.

If disease has taken hold in your organs or tissues, lycanthropy won't necessarily restore you to perfect health. Let's say you have a massive malignant tumor in your lung that has been allowed to spread unchecked. Getting bitten by a werewolf won't somehow eject those cancerous cells from your body. When you transform, that tumor will be broken down and then put back together. The process might help contain the spread somewhat, perhaps killing off some cells that are still vulnerable, but that tumor is part of your biological structure now, and when your body gets broken down, it all gets rebuilt.

The younger a person is when they are bitten, the longer they might live. A human who is bitten at age eighty will not necessarily have an extra fifty to seventy years tacked onto his life if his organs have already deteriorated beyond repair. A heart that has been ravaged by disease will be broken down and rebuilt to its same deteriorated state. The process of deterioration can be halted, but years of deterioration cannot be reversed. Going through your Moons will prevent the spread of dangerous infections or diseases that have yet to take hold, but it won't cure you after these infections and diseases have already done irreparable damage.

Make no mistake, though, your new biology is in many ways a blessing. You not only stand to live much longer, but staying healthy can require almost no effort at all.

You've Counted Your Last Carb

One of the biggest upsides of being a werewolf: you can now eat whatever you like, whenever you like. As the lycantropin goes to work on your body throughout the month, your metabolism is significantly increased, and you'll find that you have a rather formidable appetite. Carbs are burned almost as soon as they enter your system, so you'd have to be a pretty dedicated glutton to put on any weight. Just try not to make a spectacle out of yourself. If someone is already suspicious of you, their suspicions will be confirmed if you start getting kicked out of Brazilian churrascarias.

You do, however, need to make an effort to balance your diet. In both your wild and dormant states, your cravings will be for meat. An all-meat diet deprives your body of much-needed vitamins and nutrients that come from fruits and vegetables. Work non-meat items into your off-Moon meals as much as you can to try and even things out.

Exercise

Exercise, like dieting, is no longer a necessity for your new, naturally lycantropin-sculpted body. Fat is burning in your system whether you're sleeping or sprinting, and transforming back and forth during your Moons provides all the workout your muscles will need. While you won't require regular calisthenics or weightlifting to maintain your newfound physique, it is one of life's great joys to use your body and press it to its limits. Why not find out what those limits are?

Discover how many miles you can jog before getting winded. Hit the gym and check out what you can bench. Whereas before you got bitten you might have been incapable of a single pull-up, you'll now be able to do fifty of them one-handed.

Regular exercise will provide you with a sense of pride in your newfound condition, which goes a long way toward carrying you through the darker days. Additionally, you may be in much better shape than the average non-lyc, but if you ever have an altercation with another werewolf, you're going to learn that even for lycanthropes, exercise pays off.

Foreign Substances

First off, we recommend quitting smoking, drugs, and drinking to excess. While the myriad of serious health problems associated with using these substances over the long term won't really be a worry for you anymore, there still are plenty of good reasons to avoid them. We know the term "high on life" is a cliché, but now that you are suddenly able to sense the flight path of a small bird from half a mile away, pursue it through the forest at a dead sprint, and leap ten feet into the air to grab it out of the sky, you may suddenly find the kick of boozing it up or doing cocaine all night a little lacking, especially since drinking and smoking can dull these sensory experiences. Further, drinking and drugs leads to rowdiness,

---

RUN FOR YOUR LIFE!

Exercise increases the natural endorphins that make you feel better and, in many cases, allows you to sleep better too, something that (at least through the first two stages of lycanthropy) can seem like a Herculean task. Can't sleep? Haunted by either terrible nightmares or the ceaseless griping of the unwanted undead? Head out into the night for a good, hard run. You'll be surprised by how much it helps.

DON'T BELIEVE IT!
THE ONLY WAY TO KILL A WEREWOLF IS WITH
A SILVER BULLET

Every new lycanthrope always wants to know: "Will silver bullets kill me?"

Yes. They will.

However, there is absolutely no magic to it. Silver bullets will kill you not because they are silver, they will kill you because they are bullets. Try not to get shot by any kind of bullet. Bullets, in general, are bad.

---

fighting, and other more noticeable "wolfing out behaviors" (See Chapter 18, "Avoiding Detection"), which can attract the attention of werewolf hunters or the police.

Holistic Medicine and Home Remedies

It is far too dangerous for you to see an actual doctor, so studying the kinds of herbs and natural cures that exist for such day-to-day maladies as aches, pains, stomach upsets, allergies, and cuts can be very helpful, especially if you get a serious injury. If you are seriously wounded in a way that somehow fails to heal, tough it out until your next Moon, when your body will be broken down, built up, and replaced anew. In the meantime, holistic healing and home remedies can help alleviate stubborn ailments and wounds. There are many books that go much deeper into this topic, and you will find that, with some basic research, it is a snap to create your own compresses, homemade bolus suppositories, and numerous digestive aids. Now that you are becoming attuned to the natural world in a much more intimate way, discovering herbal cures can help you feel more connected to a world that may have previously left you feeling like an outsider.

PART TWO: HEALTHY MIND

Just because you don't get colds as often as other folks, don't have to worry about disease, and have enough flexibility that your bones are almost unbreakable, this doesn't mean your life will be a picnic. Far from it. Ghostly visits, nightmares, and the posttraumatic shock of not only being attacked by a werewolf, but coming to grips with turning into one can seriously hinder your mental health. And like all human beings, it's hard to have a healthy body without a healthy mind.

Embracing Routine

If you are going to live a happy life, you need to wrap your head around two things.

First, you are now living by the calendar, and that calendar is ironclad. Diabetics cannot eat candy bars, alcoholics cannot drink scotch whiskey, people who are allergic to bee stings cannot harvest their own honey, and you must be restrained or isolated every evening before, during, and after a full moon.

Second, you must embrace that routine. Really, it's not so bad once you get used to it.

Those who have made it to the Stage 4 or 5 of lycanthropy have done so by celebrating their routines and using them as templates to success. If you look at your new life as a jail sentence and count down the days to your Moon like a death row inmate counting down to his execution, your entire life will become that prison. Instead, look at your condition as a new beginning. The three days out of the month when you go through your Moons are the solid foundation upon which all of your future happiness can be built. If you do this, you will find that preparing for and safely enduring your transformations can be as rewarding as any of the other cycles of life—

EQUAL AND OPPOSITE

For every action, there is an equal and opposite reaction. Three times a month, you will transform into a savage, potentially deadly, antisocial beast. The transformation itself and your behavior as a werewolf are things you have no control over. But if you look at that loss of control as an "action," then the "equal and opposite reaction" must be a regaining of that control.

You have total control over the overwhelming majority of your life, and if it takes those three days of losing control to open your eyes to how much choice you still possess, you may come to see your lycanthropy as a blessing in disguise (a sheep in wolf's clothing?). Put simply, if you behave in a savage manner when you have no choice, you can choose to be calm when free will returns.

If it is your nature to take innocent life when you have no control, you can make a choice to nurture and embrace life the rest of the time. If you become an antisocial, violent animal when you have no choice in the matter, you can make a decision to be a good neighbor, a peaceful citizen, and a shining beacon of good grooming and hygiene when the power of choice returns. Embrace it.

from planting and harvesting to work and reward, you will discover the equal and opposite reaction to the action that your life has now taken. (See inset: Equal and Opposite.)

Building Your Calendar

Keeping a calendar can help you focus on all of the parts of your life that have nothing to do with turning into a werewolf. If you feel like your entire being is devoted to safe rooms and restraints and whatnot, a quick peek at your calendar, filled with social engagements, oil change appointments, and parent-teacher conferences, can help put things into perspective.

To start filling in your calendar, fill in your Moon Set first, and then choose at least three rest days. These scheduled rest days can be used for meditation or getting extra sleep. We recommend scheduling one of these days after the last transformation of a Moon Set and another roughly two weeks later. What you are doing is naturally counterbalancing the aggression of your Moons with the peacefulness of your hu-

June

Sun	Mon	Tue	Wed	Thu	Fri	Sat
	1	2 Initial Restraints Test	3 watch Stanley Cup	4 Second Restraints Test	5 Costco: Meat Run	6 Moon One
7 Moon Two	8 Moon Three	9 Rest Day	10 Restraint Repairs	11	12 Surfing Lesson	13 Synagogue
14 Catholic Mass	15	16	17 Sheep Delivery	18	19 poker night at Peggy and Steve's	20
21	22	23 Rest day	24 pilates	25 ref youth hockey	26 Barb's B-day party!	27 Livestock show
28 Adult ed: Stocks & Bonds	29	30 Rest day				

Phases of the moon: 7:○ 15:◐ 22:● 29:◑

manity. Those six days of the month are nonnegotiable. You can build the rest of your time upon them.

Next you should fill in chores and obligations you have to meet, such as testing and repairing restraints or shopping for materials and livestock.

Once you have filled in the things that you absolutely need to do in the short term, you can add social dates, some long-term goals, and things that you enjoy. You'll soon see that while your lycanthropy imposes a lot of demands on your time, a great deal of your month is open to you to do with as you wish.

Meditation

A major weapon in the battle against despair can be using your rest days to engage in regular periods of calm meditation. We have spoken with lycanthropes who have had good luck with the following meditation techniques, all of which can be further researched by a simple web search or a trip to a library:

1) The Koan Meditation technique, which draws from Zen Buddhism, attempts to break down the interference of the everyday world.
2) Mantra or, simply, sound techniques, which can involve anything from rhythmic chanting to singing to listening to an iPod.
3) Breathing and visualization techniques, which use controlled breathing patterns along with concentrated attempts to see yourself in your wild form and in your dormant form, and learning to define the two as one.

Misplaced Hate

It is OK to hate the monster that attacked you and made you what you are. But if you hate that monster, don't you owe it to yourself not to become him? It is the werewolf who bit you that made this happen. Not the world, not society, not God. If you believe that you are an individual with power over your own life, then it follows that the werewolf who did this to you was an individual as well. Learn from his or her mistakes the same way you learn from your own.

It's a difficult lesson, but there is truth to the fact that the werewolf who bit you is very much like a parent. He or she has not only made you what you are, but has passed along an unpleasant trait, one that you wish you didn't share. In the case of a parent, it may be alcoholism, an inability to properly express love, or even a spanking fetish. All people become their parents in certain ways, while actively avoiding others. You have been given a choice to either become like the monster that made you this way or to forge out on your own. Take the high road, and do not become what you despise.

WHAT IF I'M FEELING SUICIDAL?

Considering the quality of life available to you and the extremity of danger you pose to others, there is a very good argument to be made for a lycanthrope taking his or her own life. You will be freed of the burden of your secret. You will be freed of the extensive precautions you must take in order to avoid being discovered and, even more importantly, to avoid getting loose. And of course, the people of your city or town will be much less likely to be mauled to death if you're not around anymore.

WHY YOU WON'T KILL YOURSELF

Despite all of the rational arguments for suicide, it may surprise you to know that very few lycanthropes ever actually

Not the way to go!

kill themselves. This is due to several character traits typical of the lycanthrope, but mainly thanks to the unique cocktail of human and animal natures:

Ego. Human beings have a strong sense of curiosity and respect for their natural abilities and strengths. As a lycanthropic human, you experience such an enhancement of strength, speed, dexterity, and cunning that you will likely find it difficult not to take pride in these new abilities. Most new werewolves will be curious about what they are capable of and will want to exercise their newfound gifts.

Instinct. You're part animal now. You're a predator. While you are still human and capable of despair, you now have the self-preservation instinct of a predator. It's a strange brew, certainly, combining the wild animal's urge to hunt and kill with the human's propensity for guilt and self-analysis. But it takes a lot of guilt to beat down your lycanthropic predisposition to sustain your own life.

Joy. Just as his physical prowess is enhanced, the newly re-born lycanthrope also experiences an enhancement of the senses, and from this enhancement many new lycanthropes have reported moments of unparalleled joy, as they behold the world in which they live as if for the very first time. The earth will look as if it's been colored with a wet paintbrush. Sunsets and rainstorms that you would previously have found unremarkable will now hold you in thrall of the vivid colors dancing before your eyes. The song of a bird or laughter from a schoolyard will strike you as would a symphony. These moments will, of course, come less frequently the longer you live as a lycanthrope and grow more used to your perception, but by then you will also likely feel a little less lost in your new existence, and your suicidal ideation will have dissipated.*

DON'T BELIEVE IT!
WEREWOLF VICTIMS IN LIMBO

Killing yourself will have no effect on any afterlife passage of your victims. If you've killed and you have either dreamed or experienced a visit by the spirit of your victim, and in the visit you were told that you must commit suicide or your victim will be forced to walk in limbo between the spirit worlds forever, *DON'T BELIEVE IT!* Refer back to Chapter 7, "Werewolf Dreams and Stranger Things," for more on this, but there is no reason to believe that these encounters are anything but manifestations of a lycanthrope's guilt.

---

*Some point to this condition as evidence of the lycanthrope having a place in the evolutionary progression of life on earth. The physical enhancement of the senses heightens the lycanthrope's enjoyment of life on earth and battles his inclination to destroy himself. Had this naturally occurring biological enhancement not been present in the lycanthrope, the species would have been far less likely to survive.

PART THREE

KEEPING SECRET,
KEEPING SAFE,
STAYING ALIVE

CHAPTER SEVENTEEN

So You've Attacked Someone

Local legend said that Shady Hill Cemetery was haunted.

All the town's kids were terrified of the place. For a couple of years, that made it the perfect place to have a Moon. I had a job as a volunteer caretaker. Go in during the day, tie a sheep to a tree, come back at dusk, and boom—five square miles of open graveyard, ten miles from town. I'd eat the sheep, howl at the moon, and nobody came anywhere near. I could run around, since it was even fenced off from the main road. It was perfect . . . until I killed a couple of kids . . . thirteen, maybe fourteen years old. Two boys. They never found the bodies. I made sure of that. Should they have been there at night? Hell no. Do I blame the parents? The kids? I can't. Not anymore. It's my fault. It's like motorcyclists say, it's not if you crash your bike, it's when. If you ride a motorcycle every day of your life, sooner or later you will fall off. But it's how well you prepare for that eventuality that can either save a life or snuff one out. I see the boys from time to time. They visit me.

Local legend still says that Shady Hill is haunted. But now it haunts me.

—B.L., Auto Dealer
Age: 41, Lyc age: 9

SO YOU HAVE ATTACKED SOMEONE

It happens.

This chapter is not intended to help you justify your actions, merely to help you deal with the consequences.

Accidents do happen, and as a starting point, we will go ahead and make the assumption that the attack was just that: an accident you deeply regret.

If it was not an accident, if you don't regret it, or if you're simply unwilling to examine and change the behavior that led to the attack, you are going down a very dangerous path, one that will earn you nothing but lethal enemies, in both the lycanthropic and non-lyc communities. (For more on this see Chapter 23, "The Dark Side of Lycanthropy.") We must stress in the strongest possible terms that we condemn intentionally killing other humans or transmitting lycanthropy. These incidents do serious harm to the entire community of peaceful, responsible werewolves the world over. While the vast majority of werewolves are people who make every effort to manage their conditions safely, it only takes one ugly attack to poison the well for generations. And angry mobs don't make distinctions between good and bad werewolves.

ASSESSING THE DAMAGE

Guilt is a luxury you can indulge in later. You must first take immediate emergency action to ensure your survival.

How Many People Did You Attack?

In your early years of lycanthropy, your memories from your Moons will be hazy at best, so you must engage in a thorough investigation to determine the number of people you have attacked, as each victim can provide clues that might lead back to you.

Check the news. Pay close attention to your local television news for a story of any murders or assaults from the night of your Moon. Also, your local newspaper will probably have a crime blotter listing all the crimes in your area that police responded to.

Exactly the tip a werewolf hunter is looking for

Follow your nose. You can track your previous night's activities using your sense of smell. In your wild state, you leave your werewolf scent on everything you touch. With your heightened sense of smell, if shouldn't be hard to follow it.

Check your stool. Go through your droppings, both wolf and human. Yes, this is disgusting, but if you have attacked more than one person, you may find important clues there. In one known instance, a werewolf found his victim's wallet in his stool the next day, and he was able to immediately identify the victim by his driver's license.

Do what you gotta do

Were There Any Witnesses?

Live witnesses of werewolf attacks aren't as big a problem as you might think. Witnesses have reported werewolf attacks as everything from bear or large dog attacks—which isn't much of a stretch—to attacks by alligators or tiny hurricanes. Sometimes they even claim they saw victims struck by cars. Because people have such trouble believing in werewolves, having a witness can often be helpful, as it will usually send police down the wrong trail.

Don't Try to Clean Up the Crime Scene

You should not try to conceal or dispose of whatever is left of the bodies. After a werewolf attack, the crime scene is grisly, and it looks like the aftermath of an animal attack. This is good for you. But if you decide to violate the crime scene and conceal or dispose of the remains, you will be doing so in your dormant state, leaving behind clues that could send police to your front door. It's much safer to leave the scene of the attack as is. It's also a good idea to begin making preparations to leave town. You may have to do so, and quickly.

Are Your Victims Alive or Dead?

If your victim is dead, you are in most cases better off sticking around town. Obviously, if you have killed so many people that you are in immediate danger, get out of Dodge. But if you were fairly restrained in your rampage, don't panic. The police will more than likely be looking for a wild animal on the loose, and you probably won't even be questioned. However, if it gets reported in the press as anything that hints at a werewolf attack, it could draw the attention of werewolf hunters and the government.

If your victim survived, you have bigger problems. You must assume that the survivor has become a Stage 1 lycanthrope, and that he will be experiencing his first Moon roughly thirty days from the attack. Your victim poses a grave danger to you, the people of your town, and himself. It's up to you to help him go through his first change safely.

YOU BIT IT, YOU BOUGHT IT

The Responsibilities You Have When You Create a New Lycanthrope

If you attacked someone and they survived, congratulations, Dad! You just brought another werewolf into the world!

Just as you're responsible for your own actions, you are also responsible for any loss of life or damage caused by your creation. An uninformed Stage 1 lyc in your town is not just a threat to your neighbors, it is a threat to you and your privacy. If the town experiences a string of werewolf attacks, it will lure werewolf hunters to the area, and after enough attacks the townspeople might finally get wise and decide to hunt some werewolves of their own. For your own safety, you have to do what you can to school the new kid in the ways of the wolf.

Warn your victim. You don't want to come right out and confront them in person, since you still need to keep your condition a secret, but at the very least you should anonymously deliver this manual to your victim, along with a note warning them of what they are about to become. Be sure none of this can be traced to you.

Monitor your victim. Spy on your victim to see if he appears to be preparing for his Moon. If he is, you can rest comfortably that he's taking his new condition seriously. Chances are that he is not, which means he'll probably be running loose at the next Moon if something isn't done.

More urgent warnings. If you've already given your victim a copy of this manual, you can continue to write to your victim, pleading with him to read Chapter 5, "Tips on Your First Transformation." You can even send him a shopping list and cash necessary to purchase all the items he needs for a safe Moon.

Abduction. If your victim is still clearly not getting ready for his Moons, you can knock him unconscious and strap him down yourself. Though when you set him free the next day, you'll have to let him in on your secret. It's dangerous, but so is letting a lyc run free on his Moon.

Mentoring. This should be coupled with abduction, since you'll need your victim's undivided attention before he'll be convinced of what you're trying to get across to him. Lyc mentoring should continue beyond the first Moon, so that you can help the new lyc make the changes to his life that are necessary to his keeping safe and healthy.

Famous Lycs Through Time

Hume Cronin and Jessica Tandy, Actors

Cronin: 1911–2003, Lyc yrs: 1930–2003; Tandy: 1909–94, Lyc yrs: 1941–94

The couple met while shooting a film on location. Cronin got loose and bit Tandy, then proceeded to school her in the ways of lycanthropy. They were married soon after.

Leave town. This is a last resort. If you're not willing to devote the time necessary to prevent the new lyc from getting loose, leaving town might be the best bet. You shouldn't live in a place where people think a werewolf is on the loose. We maintain that attempting to directly restrain and instruct the new lyc is a far more practical and desirable option. No one could blame you for running away, though it is, of course, an extremely destructive surrender of the life you've built for yourself.

At the very least, please deliver a copy of this manual to your victim before you go.

Important: Murdering your victim is not an option. You should not even entertain this idea. There is a very big difference between murdering someone while in your dormant state and killing someone when you're wild. A werewolf attack looks like the work of an animal, and the police will probably not assume the assailant was human. If you kill in your dormant state, the police will go looking for you, and you could leave a trail for them. Unless you've become a criminal mastermind, there's no reason to assume you won't get caught. Under no circumstances should you consider murdering your victim an option.

WHAT DOES THE COMMUNITY THINK?

You want to be one step ahead of any panic that occurs, so you need to find out exactly how your neighbors and fellow citizens are reacting to the attack(s). Do they believe it was the work of an animal or some deranged drifter whom the police can apprehend, or do they believe it was the work of . . . something else?

Be one step ahead of the wolf hunt

Go Where They Gather

Don't just ask people what they think—listen both to what they say and what they don't say. Go to where people gather, in bars, cafés, or in the break room at work, and listen in on conversations. If they speak openly about the attacker as if it was a man, then they suspect nothing more than that. If they seem tight-lipped about the murders or cautious about discussing who or what might have been responsible, then they might be on their way to accepting that something unknown was responsible. The unknown is one of the most terrifying things for people to face, and terror is a key ingredient in mobs.

Hear Their Prayers

Ultimately, the best place to determine how your neighbors are feeling is to attend their church. If they believe they are living in the presence of something they don't understand or something they consider evil, they'll tell their ministers, whose sermons will reflect the sentiments of the congregation. If the people believe they need to hunt down a beast living in their town, you'll hear about it at their place of worship. History shows that witch hunts usually begin on the church steps. So do werewolf hunts.

Punishment Versus Reform

If you have killed or if you have passed on this condition to another, you may feel compelled to punish yourself. The guilt you feel may be so intense that you almost crave punishment as though it were an addictive drug.

Remember, this incident happened when you were wild. A wild werewolf is a dangerous and unpredictable creature, and there is nothing you can do to change that fact. Seeing as the only thing you can control is not getting loose next time, if you want to sentence yourself to hard labor, build a better restraint system.

Unlike the majority of prisoners who are locked up for committing violent crimes, you can shape your punishment in such a way as to be the executor of your own reform. You have made a mistake, you have lost control, and you have shattered lives. Now what are you going to do about it? What are you going to do about it every day for the rest of your life? How will you change your life? How will you give aid and comfort to those who have been affected by your mistakes? You must reform your behavior and, in the process, reform your soul.

CHAPTER EIGHTEEN

Avoiding Detection

I didn't start peeing on stuff until about my fourth month, when I was starting to get a little more comfortable and even a little proud. One day I just got up from my desk and starting peeing on the floor by the trash can. Luckily it happened while I was working late, and I snapped out of it after just a few seconds, but I spent the next hour scrubbing and the rest of the night trying to figure out how to control this.

Werewolves don't have masters to swat them with a newspaper, so you have to train yourself. I thought of all kinds of physical pain I could inflict on myself, my self-inflicted newspaper-swat, but I knew that wouldn't work. So instead I took to fasting. Every time I pee where I shouldn't or I howl or do something else that might compromise my identity, I go twenty-four hours without eating afterwards. It really helps me to meditate on the behavior. When you're depriving yourself of sustenance, all you can do is concentrate on the reason why.

—Tung N., Human Resources Administrator

Age: 30, Lyc age: 4

KEEPING THE SECRET IS A NEVER-ENDING TASK

OK. You've perfected a foolproof system of the most durable restraints in the most soundproof and fortified safe room that could ever be constructed by man (or, at least, half-man). You are now able to imagine a full and satisfying life lived for years and years without any foreseeable complications. You can coast now, right?

Wrong.

As a lycanthrope, you don't just need to protect others from yourself. There are many people in the world who want you dead, locked up, or dissected and experimented upon. You need to keep your identity a secret. This chapter will address precautions you need to take to avoid being found out.

WHO ARE YOU HIDING FROM?

The short answer is: everyone. But here's a list of people and groups who pose a threat to you if your secret is found out:

1. **Your community.** If your community learns about you, they'll try to drive you out of town, or worse. They just want to protect their families. Nothing personal.
2. **The police.** Never get locked up for any reason. If the police are after you, you are much better off going on the run than letting them take you into custody and risk your undergoing a Moon in a jail cell. (See Chapter 19, "Government and Police.")
3. **The government.** Again, this is covered more extensively in Chapter 19, but the American government has a history of engaging in lycanthrope "research," and that is one study you would never want to volunteer for. Don't draw the attention of the government.
4. **Werewolf hunters.** They want to kill you. Whether for vengeance or for sport, werewolf hunters are looking for you. Throw them off your trail. (See Chapter 22, "Werewolf Hunters.")
5. **Fur chasers.** Unbalanced people who want to become werewolves. They're also hunting you. (See Chapter 21, "Fur Chasers.")
6. **Everyone.** Can't be stressed enough. The safest way to

avoid detection is to let no one in on the secret. You're probably going to end up telling a loved one or two, but keep the circle of trust very small. The more people who know, the more danger you're in.

THE RULES OF AVOIDING DETECTION

Tell No One

Tell no one about your condition unless you absolutely have no choice and you know the person can be trusted, and even in such a case, try lying first and see if that works. The minute someone finds out you're a werewolf, your life is in danger.

Avoid Medical Treatment

If you become injured or ill, wait several days to see if the symptoms disappear on their own. Your regenerative powers are strong, and most ailments and injuries will heal on their own. You want to avoid doctors, hospitals, or any treatment that might require a blood sample. You don't want anyone analyzing your blood or chemical makeup.

Stay Groomed

As detailed in Chapter 2, "How to Determine If You Are Really a Werewolf," you are likely going to grow new hair patterns and experience rapid fingernail growth. Keep it all shaved and trimmed. You might feel inconvenienced by your new, rigorous grooming requirements, but it's important that your appearance not appear too radically changed.

Watch Your Behavior Patterns

You want to switch things up as much as possible to avoid anyone recognizing a pattern. If there is only one store in your vicinity where you shop for hardware and restraints, make

Keep the nails trimmed

sure to shop there on a regular basis for items completely un-related to your lycanthropy. If you drive to a safe room for your Moons, always use a different route to get there and park your vehicle far away from the location so you can be sure you weren't followed. Put the lights in your house on a timer so they automatically switch on and off to make it look like there is activity in your home during your Moons.

Watch Your "Wolf-Outs"

As mentioned in Chapter 2, "wolf-outs" are the sudden man-ifestations of wolflike "animalizations" in your dormant state. These new behaviors must be kept in check in order to avoid the attention of those watching for such behaviors. Basically, these will include howling, circling, sniffing stuff, and peeing on stuff.

Howling is a kind of exclamation. It might happen when you're excited or celebratory or engaged in an energetic dis-cussion, and you burst forth with a short, loud howl. It will happen where you might normally have laughed. It will obvi-ously attract attention to anyone looking for signs of lycs in the area, but to most other people you might just seem obnoxious. To avoid a howl, try to behave reservedly. Especially avoid drinking alcohol excessively.

Circling is the new pacing. When you're in a situation that makes you feel nervous or threatened, you might begin circling the object of your attention. It might not be apparent to anyone, even you. For example, if you're in the office and there is a new hire that you're threatened by, you might just begin walking the aisles around your office floor, keeping an eye on that new hire's desk. Or let's say you're at a party and your spouse's ex walks in. You'll keep to the walls of the party, pushing through the perimeter of the crowd and eyeing your spouse's former lover. But don't worry, you're not going to drop to all fours and attack. To the observer you'll just seem a bit restless and preoccupied. Still, it's a behavior you should keep in check.

Sniffing stuff. If anything piques your interest, from a plate of food to a new paper shredder at the office, you're going to want to lean in and give a sniff. It can be awkward, especially when you're on a first date and you keep leaning over to sniff your date's face, your date's hand, and your date's pants. Just be aware of it and try to control yourself.

Peeing on stuff. Very dangerous. This might happen when you're feeling threatened, proud, or even when you're in a new place for the first time. You go into something akin to a trance, and you just aim yourself at a spot and begin to urinate. It's very difficult to control. The best way to prevent this from happening is to make it harder on yourself. Wear pants with button flies that are difficult to unfasten. You might even wear a pair of drawstring bicycle shorts or tights under your pants, adding another difficult step to the process of freeing yourself. You won't just want to pee down your own leg; you'll want to aim your stream at a specific spot. The more difficult it is to get yourself out of your pants in order to urinate, the

DON'T BELIEVE IT!
THERE IS NO SUCH THING AS A "NATIONAL
LYCANTHROPE REGISTRY"

It might come in an e-mail requesting personal information, such as the correct spelling of your name and your address. The e-mail will claim it is asking you to update your records for the National Lycanthrope Registry, an organization it claims is devoted to the protection and advocacy of lycanthropes. The e-mail will claim that it can't devote the proper resources to your district if it has an inaccurate count of the lycanthrope population in your area. DON'T BELIEVE IT! This is a phishing-scam e-mail, a fraudulent attempt by werewolf hunters to locate gullible lycanthropes. If you receive one, don't worry that your identity has been found out. These e-mails are randomly sent to millions of addresses in the hopes that some people might take the bait and blow their cover.

more time you'll have to snap out of it before you actually go through with the act.

HOW TO MAKE SURE YOU AREN'T BEING WATCHED

We're not suggesting you spend your whole life looking over your shoulder, just part of your life. Keep an eye out for suspicious-looking people who keep popping up. Assume it's more than a coincidence.

If you've gotten loose and reports of your melee have gone out in the press, hunters might be looking for you. And even if you haven't gotten loose, there is still a chance that someone might be on to you. No matter how you draw the suspicion, you need to be aware of it when it arrives.

The Camera Doesn't Lie

Alarms will keep intruders out of your home, but they can't protect you from surveillance. To get a leg up on anyone who might be watching, you want to mount a small, discreetly placed video camera in the window of your home (and/or safe room), aimed at the street outside.

Paranoia is your friend

You don't have to record every minute of the day. If you record just the few hours between arriving home from work and going to bed, you can later fast-forward through the tape to see if there are any suspicious-looking people about or unfamiliar cars parked for long periods of time. You only need to record three or four nights a week, but change up those nights from week to week.

The three nights you must record, however, are the nights of your Moons. If someone truly thinks you are a werewolf, they are going to show up at your house (or follow you to your safe room) on the night of a full moon, regardless of the danger it puts them in. To catch them in the act, simply turn on the camera approximately an hour before nightfall and record for as long as your camera allows.

Just Keep Your Eyes Open

Be observant. Your senses are now significantly enhanced. Use them to watch your environment and look for anyone who's paying a little too much attention to you.

CHAPTER NINETEEN

Government and Police

There is no Düsseldorf Project. The federal government has never conducted experiments or inquiries concerning lycanthropy.
—State Department Official, commenting on the 1984 publication
of *The Düsseldorf Project: The Pentagon's Attempt to Enlist the Werewolf*
by Hollis Colesberry

GOVERNMENT TESTS

There are many horror stories that lycanthropes pass along to one another about government abduction of and experimentation on werewolves. Some are fictional and, sadly, some are very much based in fact. The following is a brief overview of the government's research into lycanthropy and the reasons why lycanthropes should avoid the attention of the government at all costs.

VANISHING VICTIMS

In the year 1968, the crime blotter in the *Baltimore Sun* featured three similar reports over the course of seven months. On March 13, 1968, Leopold Colvin was reportedly hitchhiking when he was "attacked by a large, wild dog," just before getting hit by a car. Leopold survived the car crash, but the dog that attacked him was never found.

Three weeks after the attack, Leopold Colvin was reported missing by his family.

On May 11, 1968, Moira Felke was reportedly the victim of an attempted rape. Peter Hollingsworth heard what sounded like "growling" and "a struggle" in his yard and went outside with his rifle. Hollingsworth claimed that from his porch he saw a woman underneath what looked like "some kind of bear." He fired one shot at the bear, and only when he got closer did he see that the attacker he'd just shot and killed was not a bear, but a naked male named Henry Vasiliadis, age forty-one. Moira Felke suffered some lacerations and bruising.

Moira Felke's husband reported her missing to the police on June 1, 1968, exactly three weeks after her attack.

On July 11, 1968, Kevin Randolph was camping in Scotts Cove Campground near Towson when a large wolf attacked him at his campsite. Kevin was pinned under the wolf with his left leg in the campfire, resulting in severe burns and amputation of the leg below the knee. The wolf was apparently caught in the fire as well, and suffered burns severe enough to send it running. Rangers rescued Randolph and took him to safety.

Mr. Randolph was reported missing by his parents on July 29, 1968.

These three reports occurred within four months of each other. All three victims, who had survived the attacks and were undergoing treatment, disappeared within three weeks of the attack. There was no indication that any of these individuals had planned to leave town. Nothing had been packed. Their homes did not appear to have been broken into. They seemed to have simply vanished. Following investigations by the police, the missing victims were presumed dead, but their bodies were never found.

THE DÜSSELDORF PROJECT

A dark, dark time for lycanthropy

First initiated in 1954, the Düsseldorf Project was a secret program established by the Pentagon to study the possibility of "controlled lycanthropy." Most of what is known about the project comes from a published account by one of its administrators. The project entailed the location and abduction of lycanthropes for the purpose of genetic experimentation for military use. The project was named after the city of Düsseldorf, Germany, where one of the first known instances of a lycanthrope's introduction into a military action is believed to have taken place.

Düsseldorf, 1939

As legend has it, in 1939 a young German soldier stationed in Düsseldorf was attacked by a werewolf. The soldier managed to get hold of his sidearm and fire a bullet straight into the werewolf's head. The soldier survived with just a mild bite. When the rest of the unit responded to the shooting, they found the soldier beside a naked dead man. The soldier could not explain to his commanding officer why he was forced to kill an unarmed naked man, and his talk of having been attacked by what looked like a furry beast only sounded hysterical to his questioners and did nothing to stamp out their suspicions that the soldier had engaged in a homosexual act prior to the killing. He was court-martialed and sentenced to death.

The execution was scheduled for the evening of the lycanthrope soldier's first Moon. Just as the lycanthrope was being led to the wall, he dropped to the ground screaming in pain and underwent his transformation into his wolf state. Three soldiers were killed and two were wounded before the werewolf was shot dead. The following month, those two wounded soldiers experienced their first Moons, and seven soldiers were killed, one wounded. The two werewolves ended up being shot while attacking each other. The next month, five soldiers were killed and two wounded. For nine straight months the Düsseldorf unit suffered werewolf attacks around the full moon, until finally, a werewolf attack ended with a dead lycanthrope and zero wounded. In all, forty-one soldiers were killed in Düsseldorf by werewolf attacks.

Washington, D.C., 1954

The Pentagon's Düsseldorf Project tried to determine whether the carnage of Düsseldorf in 1939 could be replicated in a controlled assault on a larger scale. The military wanted to learn the nature of lycanthropy in order to harness its power in the genetic manufacture of a supersoldier. The project was the brainchild of Dr. Ezra Hull, who petitioned the Pentagon to fund the project. He finally got his backing in 1954, and soon after, lycanthropes from across the country were tracked down by searching police blotters for apparent werewolf attacks. Survivors of these attacks were abducted, observed, and eventually carved open. The Pentagon studied their blood and genetic makeup in the pursuit of several ends.

First: Could the lycanthropic agent in the blood be diluted to create a creature that had the strength, fury, and size of a werewolf, but could still retain its ability to reason and, perhaps, follow orders?

Second: How was lycanthropy transmitted from host to host? Could lycanthrope blood be useful as a stealth chemical weapon, infecting the enemy on a large scale via the water supply or a food source? If enough new lycanthropes could be born at one time, it was believed that the resulting death and chaos would tear an enemy nation apart.

Third: Could the timing of the transformation be controlled? A human who could turn into a werewolf at will could make for an excellent assassin.

There were numerous other military hypotheses tested under Düsseldorf, but the project was ultimately a failure. It is believed the project was dismantled circa 1980.

While this abominable program was the worst example of the lack of compassion that usually greets lycanthropy, much of what we know about werewolves today was born from the Düsseldorf Project. One of the project's researchers, Hollis Colesberry, published an account of his work on the Düsseldorf Project while in prison, where he is serving a life sentence for the murder of his wife.*

Colesberry's Account

Colesberry's book, *The Düsseldorf Project: The Pentagon's Attempt to Enlist the Werewolf,* was published in 1984 by Cronis Books, a small press that specialized in publishing erotica and

---

*Many lycanthropes believe that Colesberry was framed so as to discredit anything he might say about Düsseldorf, despite the overwhelming evidence of his guilt.

radical political works. Cronis Books folded in 1989, and Colesberry's book has remained out of print since.

The book paints a portrait of a secret autonomous government agency that committed unspeakable experiments upon lycanthropes. Colesberry also claims in his book that the project did not limit its experimentation to lycanthropes. Non-lycanthrope humans (usually vagrants and prostitutes) were also abducted to act as control subjects in transference studies.

The fact that the Düsseldorf Project has been shut down should not ease the nerves of any lycanthrope. It certainly wasn't terminated in an act of conscience. The project was killed due to lack of any results to justify funding. Since the government still denies it ever existed, there is no reason to assume such a project couldn't be resurrected. It is essential that lycanthropes avoid being detained by any authority that has the jurisdiction to hold a citizen in custody for any period of time. Should your lycanthropy be discovered while in custody, not only will your safety and freedom be at risk, you might help initiate a large-scale effort to study lycanthropy, which could turn the entire race of lycanthropes into lab rats.

LYCANTHROPES SHOULD AVOID CRIMINAL ACTIVITY

As a lycanthrope, you can't risk getting arrested. For non-lycanthropes, being held a night in jail is a scary thing, but it happens. For you, it's potentially lethal (especially for your cellmates). You transform into a werewolf thirty-six nights out of the year, more than an entire month. If you are locked up during a Moon, assuming you don't get shot to death, you will most certainly be turned over to federal authorities.

Even though you may lead a lawful life, there are numerous situations that can arise and put you on the wrong side of

EXCERPT FROM *THE DÜSSELDORF PROJECT: THE PENTAGON'S ATTEMPT TO ENLIST THE WEREWOLF* BY HOLLIS COLESBERRY

At that point, all test subjects' fingers and toes had been amputated. If the lycanthrope's digits are removed while in its human state, we discovered, they don't develop claws when they change. We'd perfected our restraints, but even if you strap down a werewolf on an operating table, it's very dangerous to get close enough to the table to operate if it's got claws.

Dr. Hull wanted to weigh and examine the internal organs of the werewolf during its Moon, but this was next to impossible since upon death the werewolf was shown to transform back into a near-human state in as little as thirty seconds. This led Dr. Hull to conduct what could only be described as a live autopsy.

We administered general anesthetic, just enough to keep the werewolf weak but never enough to fully knock it out. After several attempts to keep the werewolves unconscious resulted in death and post-mortem transmogrification before the procedure could be completed, Dr. Hull demanded that the subject's state of unconsciousness go no deeper than significant muscle weakness to mitigate struggle, but it was clear that the werewolf felt everything. The slicing of the skin. The prying apart of the rib cage. The tugging on its internal organs. We kept the werewolf in a deep enough haze that it couldn't lift its head, but we could only reduce its howl to a loud whimper.

Most of the study had to occur while the organs were still in the subject's body. Dr. Hull would slice into their structures and peer inside, taking photographs and occasionally removing tissue, which he would then drop into a crystallization compound so as to prevent it from decomposing to its human form after removal from the body. All the while, the werewolf whimpered in pain. When it came time to actually weigh the organs, the window of time was very small. Dr. Hull had to yank the organ from the body and get it on the scale in one motion. Once the organ was on the scale we recorded the weight, then watched the number drop as the organ quickly lost its weight and girth. They seemed to deflate like punctured beach balls.

It was that day that we learned the werewolf's heart weighs approximately 3.8 pounds, or about five times the size of the human heart.

the police. A bar fight, for example. If someone takes a swing at you, don't swing back. In fact, you should leave the premises before a second swing can even be thrown. When the cops show up to break up a fight, they don't always take the time to find out who started it. They could haul you both away to cool off at the station.

No driving drunk, even when you think you're under the limit. No public drunkenness. No buying marijuana or any other illegal drugs. No public urination.

Be a Good Citizen

Pay your taxes. And avoid itemized deductions if you can. If there is a hunt for lycanthropes under way, a great place to look would be at purchase patterns on tax forms that might raise red flags. So when you buy those straps and steel rods to build your safe house restraint system, don't try and write it off as a business expense. Bite the bullet.

Avoid political extremism. Obviously you should avoid public demonstrations where you would run the risk of being arrested. But you should also keep from being identified as an associate of any organizations that might attract the attention of authorities. We're not saying the government is constantly using satellites to watch every American who ever attended an antiwar rally. But the fact is, known members of radical organizations can find their names added to a file at some point. Your goal is to keep your name from being added to those files to the greatest extent possible.

Never accept government employment. The pension is great, but once you accept their paycheck, your entire life is an open book.

Never give anyone your blood. You should avoid physicians at all costs, and you should never have your blood studied by a doctor. But if you must, pay well for the private care. A subsidized health office or clinic is one that is beholden to the government, and you cannot be sure of the information-sharing that is being practiced.

Most importantly . . . don't get loose. The minute one of those "man attacked by giant dog" reports gets in the papers, a red flag is raised, and interested parties come poking around. It's the number one rule for your protection. Protecting yourself from getting loose and harming others is the most surefire way to keep yourself out of danger.

CHAPTER TWENTY

The Trouble with Vampires

They prance around like the whole universe is their own private goth dance club. And try to get 'em to talk about anything but blood. They can't think of nothing but their next vein. And they look down on everybody, but especially lycs. They think lycs are dirt, and I think they're all nothing but a bunch of smug corpses. So I guess we kind of have an understanding.

—Peter T., Horticulturalist
Age: 30, Lyc age: 15

NAVIGATING YOUR INTERACTIONS WITH THE SMUG, EFFEMINATE UNDEAD

Werewolves and vampires have a very long history together, dating back centuries. Their relationship rests somewhere on a scale between mutual hatred and grudging tolerance. According to legend, in the old days when vampires and werewolves were able to roam with much more freedom, a rivalry developed. There are many explanations for the rivalry, but at the root it seems to have been born out of a competition to determine which creature was more deadly.

These days, there is not much time to stoke rivalries, as both vampires and werewolves are too busy trying to keep a low profile. But the animosity is still very much there. Vampires see werewolves as a contaminated species of human whose blood isn't fit to drink. They look down on werewolves as graceless, vulgar, filthy dogs. Werewolves, for their part, see vampires as creepy, snobbish corpses who think they're God's gift to creation. It's a feud that won't be resolved any time soon, and the only thing you can do is try to avoid vampires as much as possible, since having to deal with one can be a real drag.

SPOTTING A VAMPIRE

You'd likely never have noticed them before you got bitten, but now that you have your enhanced sensory capabilities, you're probably stunned that you could never detect them before. They're so obviously, glaringly undead.

The first thing you'll notice is the odor. It will probably be masked by perfume or cologne, but not enough to shield you from it. Vampires smell of the grave, and the scent will hit your nose like the stink of a damp, moldy basement that has been sealed for years. If you encounter a vampire in a restaurant, you won't be able to eat there. It will smell like a room that might be crawling with germs and unchecked bacteria, and you'll worry that breathing might make you ill. Given your new grooming habits and tendency to mark your territory, you might have a distinctive odor that some find objectionable, but at least you smell alive. Vampires just smell like decay.

Next is their appearance. When you finally lay your eyes on one, you'll be stunned that he thinks he's passing as a live human. Before you were bitten, vampire skin probably just looked a little paler than you're used to seeing. Now that you're a lyc, vampire skin will look almost transparent and bruised. You'll notice the deep blue shadows in their cheeks and around their eyes, a blue as deep and dark as a summer night sky. If he smiles, his gums will either be fire engine red or light pink, depending on his last feeding. There will be no hint of wrinkles or imperfections. And of course, he will seem to carry himself with his nose held a bit high in the air.

Finally, you can spot a vampire by the way he's looking at

you. Vampires can spot lycanthropes just as easily as lycs can spot a vampire. They can smell your scent, and some can even hear the pulse of your blood flow, which pumps at a dramatically quicker pace than that of a non-lyc. He will not do anything to mask his disgust at your presence. When you enter a party, the vampire will be the one who is glaring at you as if he's wondering how you ever got invited. Do what you can to keep from walking right up to him and scratching that sour expression off his face.

WHEN IS A VAMPIRE A DANGER TO YOU?

In most circumstances when you come in contact with a vampire, the two of you will probably just glare at each other without any real conflict. If you do come to blows, it will probably be because the vampire sees you as intervening on one of his kills.

In your dormant state, if you spot a vampire who appears to have a victim under his spell (to a non-lyc, the victim will look like he or she is in love, but to you it will look more like the victim is under hypnosis), the vampire might take action to get you out of the picture. Usually, the vampire will just hasten away with his victim, but he might also threaten you or even assault you if he thinks he can get away with it. The vampire is very dangerous to you in your dormant state. He's not going to try and drink your blood, but he will try to beat you senseless and maybe even snap your neck to keep you from warning his victim of his true nature and intentions. For your own safety, when you happen upon a vampire in your dormant state, it's best to mind your own business.

Famous Lycs Through Time
McLean Stevenson, Actor
(1927–96, Lyc yrs: 1960–96)
Said to have blamed failure
of sitcom *Hello, Larry* on
Hollywood's "vampire mafia."

If you happen upon a vampire in your wild state, you might end up being the aggressor. When you're wild, the ghostly aura surrounding the vampire will frighten you but also turn you immediately hostile to his presence, and you will do all you can to chase him from the area, including waging a physical attack. The vampire will see you as competition for any human prey in the vicinity, and he will either yield the area to you or try to spook you away. Rarely will a vampire actually engage in a fight with a wild werewolf.

WHO WOULD WIN IN A FIGHT?

If you and a vampire were ever to actually have a physical altercation, you would win easily. Vampires may be undead, but they cannot survive being torn limb from limb, which is what you would do to one if he should choose to engage you. You would never hunt a vampire for food, since he does not give off the scent of flesh, only decay. The only reason the two of you would fight is if you detect him as a threat. However, it is very unlikely that a vampire would actively subject himself to an attack.

While the vampire is very strong, he does not rely on the wielding of physical brawn the way you do. The vampire's talents are seduction, trickery, and evasion. He knows that, in your wild state, you are hostile but also terrified by his ghostly presence. The vampire would try to play up that terror, stirring your fear and confusion until you run away. You're a rather simple animal when wild, and the vampire would try to confuse you until you feel that retreat is your safest bet. If that didn't work out, the vampire himself would probably choose retreat over a physical engagement. His hours out of the coffin are precious. He would rather not waste them being ripped to pieces by the likes of you.

CHAPTER TWENTY-ONE

Fur Chasers

Yeah, OK. I was into it. But there was nothing else to do in my stupid town, man. It was either play football, do drugs, or . . . be a weirdo. I was one of the weirdos and fell in with some werewolf freaks. We found out that there was a lyc living three towns over—had been for years. So the five of us broke into his house on the full moon, knocked him out, chained him up, and waited. Then we lined up and let him take a bite. He managed to take one of my friend's hands off. The next month, we all drove out into the woods and had our first Moon together. Very bad idea. Two of us didn't make it through the night.

The other two died not long after that. I'm still alive. Still managing. Still wishing I had gotten more into football.

—Lionel J., Real Estate Broker
Age 41, Lyc age: 25

WHAT IS A FUR CHASER?

A fur chaser is a non-lyc who wants to become a werewolf and goes so far as to try to be attacked by a werewolf or to steal a werewolf's fluids.

For every objectionable, repulsive, or dangerous activity imaginable, there is someone out there who's into it. The more irresponsible the behavior, the stronger some will try to embrace that behavior. It is hard to imagine that anyone would ever actually *try* to become a werewolf, but believe it or not, there are those out there who are into it.

Smitten and very dangerous

HOW DO THEY DO IT?

The most avid fur chaser is a kind of werewolf hunter who will track down a werewolf and try to come in contact with him during his Moon, or who will abduct and restrain a dormant lyc, waiting for him to transform. The fur chaser wants the lycanthrope's fluids. You may be a lycanthrope who has followed the suggestions of this book to the letter and who takes all necessary precautions during your Moon to keep restrained and safe from harming others, but you will still have to worry about being snuck up on by these maladjusted fools, who actually *want* you to hurt them.

THE FUR CHASER PERSONALITY

What Kind of Person Would Actually *Try* to Become a Werewolf?

Fur chasers are usually people who have very little going on for themselves. They generally have painfully dull personalities and were likely outcasts during their formative years. They

There's "innocent," and then there's "obsessive"

allow almost the entirety of their identities to be defined by their longing for lycanthropy. They have few friends, and their social activity is limited to Internet communities of people who share their obsession. They are not necessarily goth, though some might dabble in the occult to seek a spell or potion that is mistakenly believed to be capable of turning people into werewolves. Fur chasers never marry and rarely date. They would argue that prospective partners are put off by their lycanthropy fixation, but given their social awkwardness, it is doubtful that they would be very successful on the dating scene even if they overcame their obsession.

Many fur chasers claim to have suffered an indignity or injustice of some kind. This could be anything from being marginalized during their school years to a physical assault. They might also feel that they've been underestimated or unjustly excluded throughout their lives. Thus they are often drawn to lycanthropy from a desire for vengeance against those who've wronged them. Not that they intend to turn into werewolves and attack their enemies, but they are drawn to what they imagine to be a superhuman sense of power possessed by a lycanthrope. They imagine lycanthropy will elevate them to a superior state of being so that they can finally look down on those who've been cruel to them.

We know a great deal about fur chasers since, of all the denizens of the lycanthrope universe, these individuals were by far the most willing to be interviewed for this book, with many of them even seeking us out hoping to be included. Apparently, in the fur chaser community, inclusion in a werewolf reference manual is a kind of status achievement, and several of them argued against our policy of maintaining the anonymity of those being interviewed. Though very few fur chasers will ever become werewolves, we refuse to disclose their identities to avoid reprisals against them by werewolves who consider fur chasers to be a threat.

> **THE PERSONALITY OF A FUR CHASER**
> Low self-esteem
> Weak sense of identity
> Very few friends beyond those who share their obsession with werewolves
> Very few interests beyond their obsession with werewolves
> No romantic attachments
> No close family attachments
> Might feel victimized
> Might feel underestimated
> Dream of vengeance on those who wronged them

The Fur Chaser Who Loves You

One exception to the typically objectionable fur chaser is the one who is only interested in becoming a werewolf to be closer to a loved one. When two people love each other very much and one of those people happens to be a werewolf, the one who isn't can start to feel left out. Couples who share everything will bristle at any hint of distance from a partner. It will enter the mind of the non-lyc partner that if he or she were to be bitten, both partners would be able to share this

---

HELP RENDER THE FUR CHASER SITES USELESS

Fur chasers usually communicate online, and they maintain databases of possible lycanthrope spottings at sites like fangstalker.org. Such sites are places where fur chasers share news reports that might indicate a werewolf attack, and they work together to try to positively identify lycanthrope locations. We encourage all readers of this book to flood these sites with false reports. They are virtually worthless already, but the only way to keep them that way is if their users feel they can never tell a true report from an intentionally misleading one. Additionally, new sites often sprout up elsewhere. If you ever come upon one, start sending in false reports. It's the best way to cripple their efforts to compromise the privacy of lycanthropes.

---

experience, just as they've shared everything else. Such a person is a fur chaser in name only. They may want to become a werewolf, but only to be closer to the one they love.

This is, of course, a monumentally bad idea and should not be entertained. For more on this type of fur chasing, see Chapter 13, "Romance and the Modern Lycanthrope."

HOW DO FUR CHASERS COURT A WEREWOLF ATTACK?

The hardest part is tracking down a werewolf. One has to be very lucky (or unlucky) to find a werewolf living in his immediate vicinity, so fur chasers are usually forced to follow the same leads as werewolf hunters. They search news outlets across the country for reports of violent crimes that share the characteristics of a werewolf attack. Then they travel to see for themselves.

Once a fur chaser has discovered a lycanthrope, he will

try to come in contact with that lycanthrope during a Moon via several methods. If you keep yourself properly restrained during your Moons, the fur chaser might try to enter your safe room and get close enough to receive a bite, while keeping enough distance to avoid your grip. This is very risky, of course, since many restraints systems are designed simply to keep you from running loose, still giving you more than enough leeway to rip someone apart who places himself within biting distance. (See Chapter 10, "Strapping In.")

Since any situation involving a werewolf attack is almost guaranteed to end in death, the most common method employed by fur chasers is to assault and abduct the werewolf while he is in his dormant state. While unconscious, you would be restrained by the fur chaser in such a way that when you transform into your wild state, you will be defenseless. Once you've changed, the fur chaser will then draw your blood and inject it into his own body, thus giving himself lycanthropy. The entire process must be done during your Moon. If a non-lyc were to inject your blood later in the month, it would have no effect.

Do Fur Chasers Kill Their Werewolves After Stealing Their Fluids?

Some fur chasers will kill the restrained lycanthrope once they've gotten what they came for, but most will not. In fur chaser circles, it is considered a common courtesy to avoid killing lycanthropes unless one's life is in danger. Fur chasers implore each other to keep werewolves alive so that others might also track them down for their fluids.

WARNING SIGNS THAT SOMEONE IS A FUR CHASER

In most cases, fur chasers will try to confirm that you are a lycanthrope by observing you from afar. You should already be on the lookout for surveillance of yourself and your home. If you are being watched by anyone, it's probably bad news. (For more on this, see Chapter 18, "Avoiding Detection.")

Sometimes, the fur chaser will try to get to know you personally. They might try to establish a friendship or an affair. Remember, these people are obsessed with lycanthropes to the degree that they actually want to become one. It follows that they would want to know one as well, seeing as the lycanthrope is essentially a fur chaser's idol. You should be watchful of strangers going out of their way to make your acquaintance, especially when these strangers seem socially awkward. If they have no other friends, no apparent interests, and if their personalities are on the whole repellant, stay away from them and be extra careful in anticipation of your next Moon.

IF *YOU* ARE A FUR CHASER

Since fur chasers crave any and all lycanthropy literature, it is a sure bet that they will read this book. If you are a fur chaser, we beg you to stop in your pursuit of attaining lycanthropy. You have no right to invade the private and personal space of lycanthropes, and you have no clue what you're getting yourself into. Anyone who chooses to become a werewolf cannot possibly possess the level of maturity necessary to manage this massive burden. Lycanthropy is not something you try on *to see how it feels*. It is not a drug. It is not an exclusive club to sneak into. It is a dangerous and difficult-to-manage physical condition that must be treated with the utmost gravity. Please, please, please stop before it's too late.

TRUE LEGENDS?

THE HOST

Several decades ago a lycanthrope named Lyle lived a rather solitary existence in a remote part of West Virginia. No family, no contact with society except when needed. On his Moons Lyle kept himself chained up in the fruit cellar of his home. When he was forty-one years old, with a lyc age of eighteen, some men came to his home and abducted him.

He was taken to Budapest, where the men lived on an estate together. There were at least two dozen of them. He came to know their faces, though he did not speak their language, nor they his.

The captors observed Lyle's Moons with great ceremony. As the evening of his Moon approached, Lyle was kept restrained on an upraised altarlike table. He could not move his arms or legs, nor could he even turn his head from side to side. The men surrounded him in a circle, waiting for him to change.

He has no memory of what his captors did to him during his Moons. At every Moon he would be chained down and expect to be sacrificed, but the following morning he would awaken again, back in his cage in a basement chamber of the estate. The only thing he noticed was that each month the circle grew smaller, and that occasionally a new face would appear in the house.

After many months, an unfamiliar man appeared on the estate and began tending to Lyle in his chamber, bringing his meals and cleaning his cage. This man spoke some English, and he finally revealed what was happening to Lyle.

After Lyle would transform, they would cut him, and one man would come from the circle to drink Lyle's blood, attaining lycanthropy. The following month, that man would be gone from the circle, chained up in his own chamber. They were a fur chaser cult, and Lyle was the host, providing the lycanthropy that was spread through their cult, one man at a time, Moon after Moon.

Not long after that, Lyle began planning his escape, and his revenge. After many months the ceremonies stopped, as everyone in the house had already become lycanthropes, with no new members added to the cult. They were a house full of werewolves, and they all had to slip into their restraints during their Moons.

On the night of his escape, when the cult member arrived to strap Lyle into his restraints, Lyle opened the man's throat with his fingernails. Then he waited until there was just a half hour's time before nightfall, when everyone would be strapped in and waiting for the change. Lyle ran through the house, chamber to chamber, slitting the throats of the lycanthropes while they were strapped into their restraints but still in dormant form, so they knew exactly what was happening to them. One by one he killed them, then he set fire to the estate and ran outside just in time to transform into a werewolf and take off running for the hills.

CHAPTER TWENTY-TWO

Werewolf Hunters

Oh, they're out there. They have guns, they have technology, and worse, they have their dogma. There's no arguing with a true believer, and they want every single one of us dead. If you ask me, they're all a bunch of repressed . . . what's the term? Furries? Fur chasers? I mean, it's always the loudest anti-gay bigots who get caught tapping their toes at somebody under the bathroom stall, right? Why would an anti-werewolf bigot be any different?
—Kirk T., Blogger/Video-Store Clerk
Age: 37, Lyc age: 5

Ever since there have been werewolves, there have been werewolf hunters.

Werewolf hunters are a small but dedicated fraternity. There aren't many of them for an obvious reason: They hunt werewolves, intentionally putting themselves in direct contact with one of the most dangerous and deadly creatures on the face of the earth. In the vast majority of cases, if you show us an amateur werewolf hunter, we'll show you a bloody patch of soil on the morning after a Moon. Much like Stage 1 lycanthropes, those who try to hunt werewolves rarely survive much past their first encounter, and if they do, they only manage it with a combination of skill, obsession, and luck. But make no mistake: The ones that have managed to survive and kill multiple lycanthropes are intelligent, driven, and very, very dangerous.

They'll stalk you when you're most vulnerable

AN IMPORTANT DISTINCTION

When we talk about werewolf hunters, we don't mean someone who kills a werewolf out of self-defense or hunts a specific rogue wolf that has caused serious harm and threatens to do so again. A werewolf that lets himself get loose on his Moons is a danger to the innocent, and when the innocent are threatened, responsible citizens have every right to eliminate that threat with extreme prejudice.

Werewolf hunters make a sport out of tracking, hunting, and murdering lycanthropes of all kinds. They make no distinction between the dangerous, rogue werewolf that ravages a town month after month and those lycanthropes who might be living peaceful, responsible lives never having hurt a soul. The werewolf hunter has a dangerous obsession with lycanthropes. These hunters will pull up roots and travel the world in search of werewolves, getting a bloodthirsty thrill from capturing, torturing, and killing lycanthropes. They consider it sporting to infiltrate a lycanthrope's home and kill him, along with his family, in cold blood. It is from these hunters that you need protection.

Several lycanthropes have refused to participate in this book, some even accusing us of being werewolf hunters ourselves, for the reason that making this information public aids and abets the cause of those who would hunt them down. We reject this view. It is our heartfelt belief that any werewolf hunter who reads this book will gain insight into the personalities and struggles of the humans (yes, *humans*) that they seek to track and kill, and ultimately, abandon their quest.

DETERMINING IF A WEREWOLF HUNTER IS HUNTING YOU

First off read (or reread) Chapter 18, "Avoiding Detection." Anything out of the ordinary that might set off warning bells for a novice will certainly tip off a veteran werewolf hunter. Here are some additional things to watch out for:

Be Alert About Any Stranger Who Asks to See You on the Evening of a Moon

A common trick of werewolf hunters is to pretend to be a cable guy, phone technician, door-to-door salesmen, religious pamphleteer, or whatever, and merely knock on your door. Handle it by being noncommittal, getting a phone number, and telling them you will follow up. Investigate, if you can, from a safe distance. Unless you are dealing with a hunter who is a lyc himself (more on this later), your senses are much more highly evolved than his. Use this advantage to determine his motives. If he is a werewolf hunter, you must do everything you can to avoid or eliminate him before he does the same to you.

If It Seems Too Good to Be True, It Probably Is

If you find flyers around your community or receive e-mail blasts for ridiculously cheap livestock or meat, proceed with caution. Like most hunters, werewolf hunters use bait. In many cases, they will troll national and local media for reports of animal attacks, and when one turns up, they will paper a local community with offers that lycanthropes would find enticing. The fact that they actually advertise goods and services that appeal to the lycanthrope's desire to remain safely restrained through their Moons is evidence enough that these people are less interested in keeping a community safe than they are in lycanthrope genocide.

Steer Clear of Strangers on Horseback As Well As Certain Dog Breeds

Werewolf hunters exploit horses' natural fear of werewolves by riding through public spaces on horseback. They also employ dogs that either have been given a scent at the scene of an attack or simply have been trained to detect lycanthropes. While there is no guarantee as to which dogs have been trained to detect lycanthropes, we urge particular caution when observing the following breeds of dogs: Bouvier des Flandres, German shepherd, Maltese terrier, Shetland sheepdog, or toy poodle.

As a side note, if you see a dog that raises an internal alarm, trust your instincts. If you can get the dog alone, often merely locking eyes with it and giving a sharp growl can establish your dominance. Despite your human appearance, you are the much bigger dog. If you can communicate your alpha status in a way that will not be noticed by its handler, you may find that a potential threat can become an ally.

Popular werewolf hunting dogs to watch out for

BOUVIER DES FLANDRES

MALTESE

GERMAN SHEPHERD

SHETLAND

POODLE

WHO TO LOOK OUT FOR

While there are many different types of people who might pursue werewolves, most werewolf hunters fall into a handful of categories, detailed below.

The Religious Nut

Generally, werewolf hunters who have been "called by God" to hunt werewolves are the easiest to deal with. In many cases, they will attempt to win over supporters at the local church that is the closest to their own personal faith, and usually come off as pretty radical. In churches, gossip always holds sway, and if someone comes in from out of town and starts a lot of talk about "hunting down demons" or "eliminating the hounds of hell," people talk about it. If you live in

This won't end well

a community that isn't prone to fringe religions, cults, or excessive superstition, this type of hunter will likely be shunned by the community or even driven to the county line by the local police and told politely but firmly to "move along."

Religious nuts also tend to confront lycanthropes on the night of their Moon, relying just on their faith or, perhaps, a cross to keep them safe from harm. With all due respect to religions of every stripe, this tactic has a very low survival rate. As mentioned in Chapter 18, "Avoiding Detection," keeping an eye and ear close to the activities of the local houses of worship is always a good idea.

The Revenge-Seeking Vigilante

This is the type of hunter who has lost a loved one, often a spouse, a child, parents, or all of the above. They deal with this loss not merely by hunting the lycanthrope who killed

THE MENTOR

One subset of revenge-seeking vigilantes are known as "mentors," single men or women who hunt werewolves with a child or young adult protégé in tow. The mentor title is certainly tongue-in-cheek, as this kind of individual is a positive role model to no one. It is very likely that this child has been told he or she is an orphan of a werewolf attack. While in some cases this may be true, in most cases it is not and is an attempt by these bereaved werewolf hunters to repair their broken families. It is not uncommon for a werewolf hunter of this kind to have abducted the child. If you suspect that a hunter of this kind is on your trail, it is a good idea to anonymously tip the press or police, asking them to look into the background of the child. If the investigation shows an improper relationship with the child, which it almost certainly will, the authorities may get this "mentor" off your back for you.

their loved one, but by waging war against lycanthropes everywhere. While your heart may go out to this type of werewolf hunter initially, it is important to remember that he or she is not only blaming you for a crime you did not commit, but willing to execute you for it. The key way to identify these hunters is that they tend to be far sloppier than other kinds of hunters, often letting their grief get in the way of their better judgment. These revenge seekers will take more personal risks than other, more dispassionate hunters. In short, they are less skilled than some hunters, but far more driven.

Self-Hating Lycanthropes

These are the second-most dangerous type of werewolf hunters, as they are werewolves themselves, with the same heightened senses and reflexes you have, but in most cases

HOW TO DETECT A SELF-HATING
LYCANTHROPE HUNTER

Remember: it's better to have a non-lycanthrope friend do the asking, and to make sure they don't ask these questions all at once. These questions could alarm the self-hater, and the last thing you want to do is get a lycanthrope upset or suspicious, especially one who may be capable of murder.

STEP ONE: Expose their hatred of excess hair growth.

Sample question: Nice haircut! Where'd you get it?

Self-haters are obsessed with their grooming. While it is important that all lycanthropes get a handle on their hygiene, self-haters go above and beyond, often scheduling beauty appointments the first day after their Moons are over. Since they love to talk about how well-coiffed they are, they are happy to let you know where they get their hair cut, and potentially several reasons why it is the best place in town. Swing by their hair salon sometime and chat up the secretary. If you can finesse yourself a look at their scheduling book, try and find out when your suspect is getting haircuts. If they are happening on the days after Moon Sets, that is a very telling clue.

STEP TWO: Expose their hatred of red meat.

Sample question: Hey, where can a fella get a good steak in this town?

In many cases, self-hating lycanthropes will claim to be vegetarians, or even vegans. As they associate meat-eating with their lycanthropy, they will likely be repulsed at the mere mention of red meat.

STEP THREE: Expose their hatred of bodily functions.

Sample question: Is there a restroom nearby, or should I just head behind the nearest tree?

Seeing as all lycanthropes go through a natural urge to mark their territory with urine, the idea of urinating in any place other than a sanitary toilet (and sometimes even then) is unbearable for any self-hater to consider, and the mere mention of urinating outside will often produce a visceral reaction of horror, a clear warning sign.

STEP FOUR: Expose their hatred of the moon and, by association, nighttime.

Sample question: You catch *Conan* last night?

The self-hater is so upset by becoming a werewolf at night that he will often develop a hatred of night itself and tend to claim that he is "always in bed by ten" or a "total morning person." In addition, he will often attempt to suggest that the reason other people like to stay out late at night is because they are lazy or stupid.

Something to remember: just because someone is a compulsively well-groomed vegetarian who has bathroom issues, keeps an early bedtime, and wears way too much perfume or deodorant, that does not automatically make him a self-hating werewolf hunter.

But it's worth watching out for.

much further along in development, giving them the tactical edge. These lycs are gripped by a bizarre psychosis in which they are aware they are lycanthropes but hate it intensely, often thinking they are irredeemably evil. But rather than doing the work to accept themselves and their own limitations, they set out to eradicate others like them from society. This allows them to feel justified in whatever murderous activity they engage in (either in human or wolf form) because, in their view, eliminating as many lycanthropes as possible allows them to remain werewolves, as their evil behavior is cancelled out on balance. The best way to detect these hunters is to use your sense of smell, along with a series of pointed questions.

While all lycanthropes can generally detect each other through smell, self-haters see their natural scent as a filthy odor to be concealed and often use excessive amounts of perfume or deodorant to conceal it. Detecting someone who is obviously masking their scent can be a valuable clue to their presence.

The Rare-Breed Sportsman

While very rare, this type of werewolf hunter is the most dangerous, as they generally target lycanthropes in human form, abduct them, and transport them to a place of their choosing for the transformation, either to hunt you, imprison you, or even force you to fight other lycanthropes.

These hunters are extremely wealthy. They have been hunting large, dangerous wild animals all their lives, garnered an impressive collection of trophies, and now seek increasingly exotic game. The rare-breed sportsman will usually hunt a lycanthrope who has been kidnapped from his home and let loose in a hunting preserve or other contained grounds.

These hunters will often pursue their game with a sense of sportsmanship. They will never hunt a lycanthrope in his dormant state. They will often refuse to kill a werewolf while he is eating. Rare-breed hunters will often refuse to hunt with a rifle scope or, on occasion, will use only a bow and arrow. It's said that some unhinged hunters have pursued their werewolf prey armed only with a knife and club, though it's doubtful any such hunters have lived to tell their tale.

CHAPTER TWENTY-THREE

The Dark Side of Lycanthropy

I thought I was an agent of the apocalypse. Around the autumn of 1999, when everyone was worried about the world ending and computers crashing and just generally freaking out, I got loose and mauled a guy. Father of two young daughters. He had to be identified by dental records, I chewed so much of his face off the skull. In the months following that, I convinced myself that I was probably just one little cog in the apocalyptic machine, and there was probably heinous shit going on all over the globe that would make me look like an angel by comparison. I started thinking maybe there's no real reason to contain my Moons anymore, that the whole castle was coming down. But then the New Year passed and the world didn't end and I realized I was just a lyc who had a loose Moon and killed an innocent man. I guess I couldn't handle it and was looking for an excuse to sidestep the guilt. Luckily I came around before I became a real danger.

—Maria T., Physical Therapist
Age: 46, Lyc age: 12

WHEN GUILT GOES WRONG

Arguably the most important precaution a lycanthrope can take involves appropriately managing his emotional and mental state in the weeks and months following an attack.

When you wake up after a loose Moon and discover that you've just murdered an innocent civilian, you're going to have a whole lot of guilt to process. The goal is to accept that this sort of thing happens, and the only thing you can do is try harder not to get loose next time. No one's saying the guilt over that kill will ever go away, but the best you can do is accept the burden of that guilt and try to be safer next time.

In the face of carrying that burden, you might try to embrace some pretty dark rationalizations. "I'm a monster," you might think. "No point in fighting it anymore." Monsters, after all, don't bother with guilt.

When you reach out into the darkness to explain away your kill, it can lead to some terrifying ends. Here are some ways that lycanthropes tend to surrender themselves to darkness.

ON A BLOOD MISSION FROM GOD (THE CHOSEN WOLF)

You might decide to agree with many non-lycanthropes that you are doing the work of God and/or the devil, and therefore

You really think he has nothing better to do than watch you eat his children?

anyone who has a problem with your kills should take it up with their rosary. It's much easier to explain your condition away as a tool of Satan or divine justice rather than the biological process that it really is. If Satan or God cursed you with this fate in order that you might carry out either of their plans for humanity (plans that would appear to amount to little more than "some of humanity will be eaten"), then you certainly can't be blamed for what you do on your Moons.

This is usually coupled with the development of a fierce religiosity, as you begin to feel that you have been specially selected to do the bidding of a higher power. The belief that God or the devil is working through you also allows you to make peace with the fact that you will likely be dead soon, since you're letting yourself run free on your Moons. Nothing to worry about. God will look after you in the next world, right?

EMBRACE THE CHAOS (SPORT KILLING)

On the opposite end of the spectrum, you might decide that you are living proof that the world is godless and completely devoid of any moral or ethical code. If human biology is such that a man can thrice a month want nothing more than to hunt and feed upon his fellow man, apparently humankind isn't all that special. What room is there for morality when your instincts are no different than those of a shark in the water? Might as well embrace your fate and be the beast that nature expects of you. This is the sort of thinking that can lead a lycanthrope to engage in what is known as "sport killing."

Sport killing is where the lycanthrope plans for his Moons to take place in locations where the utmost blood can be spilled. This sort of lycanthrope has resigned himself to the fact that there really is no such thing as good or evil. He believes the world is ruled by chaos and has decided to embrace his role as an agent of chaos in the same way the zealot lycanthrope embraces his role as an agent of God. In the case of the sport-killer, he revels in this role and tries to see just how much havoc he can wreak upon the world.

In reality, there's nothing "sporting" about it

Sport-killers will have their Moons in shopping malls or amusement parks or in the audience of a summer blockbuster movie. The sport-killer werewolf sees his Moon as the chance to teach the populace a lesson about how random and inconsequential human life is. Mostly though, the sport-killer wants to see just how powerful a deliverer of death he can be. His hope is that he will live through his Moon to find out the next day how many he killed. But if he dies, so be it. His life (and death) is no more special than the lives of all those he hopes to kill. He imagines himself going out in a bloody blaze of glory, tearing apart a populace with fangs and claws.

---------------- **TRUE LEGENDS?** ----------------

ANA FLIGHT 60, FEBRUARY 4, 1966

All Nippon Airways (ANA) Flight 60 was a Boeing 727-81 aircraft that had departed from Sapporo-Chitose Airport on the day of February 4, 1966, carrying 133 souls (126 passengers, 7 crew). One of those passengers was Jiro Kuroki, a landscaper and, if his sons are to be believed, a werewolf.

Kuroki died that day, along with all 133 people on that flight, when the plane crashed into Tokyo Bay just six miles from Tokyo's Haneda International Airport, their arrival location. The plane reportedly began its descent at approximately seven p.m., and then just continued descending until it crashed into the bay. The aircraft disintegrated on impact and sank. According to the Aviation Safety Network, the probable cause of the crash was not determined.

Two important details. First, the weather that evening was clear. Second, in 1966, the full moon fell on February 5. Therefore, if Jiro Kuroki was a werewolf, he boarded that flight knowing that he was getting on a commercial airliner on February 4, the first Moon of the month, and that the plane would not be landing until just after nightfall.

Was Jiro Kuroki the cause of this aircraft's premature descent into the bay? Did he transform into his wolf state just minutes before the plane was scheduled to land, wreak havoc in the cabin, perhaps attack the cockpit, and send the plane down into the water below?

His two sons believe the answer is yes. They say that their father had never gotten beyond his grief over his wife's death two years prior. She was killed in an accident involving their father's lawn shears, they were told. They say he had grown dark and distant ever since she passed. He was flying that day after a visit to her grave (she was buried at a church near her Hokkaidō birthplace).

After his death, the sons went to his home to gather his possessions. That is when they say they discovered an ornate restraint mechanism concealed in his dressing area. They weren't sure what to make of it at first, but after some research they realized that their father might have been a lycanthrope, and that when their mother died, it might not have been a landscaping accident. The Kuroki boys believe their father killed their mother, likely by accident during a Moon, and thereafter he slowly lost his mind until he boarded a crowded airplane knowing full well he would be turning into a werewolf while the plane was still in midair.

SUICIDE BY MOON

Sometimes when a lycanthrope decides to stop restraining himself during his Moons, what he's really doing is passively planning his own suicide. Lycanthropes certainly have more than enough supporting arguments to justify a suicide attempt, and many make an attempt long before they harm someone. The desire to end it all might grow much stronger if you've gotten loose and killed someone. The guilt might be too much for you to take, and you might want to do yourself in. You might even see your own death as penance for those you've killed. So you'll follow any line of thinking that makes your getting loose an inevitability, knowing that if you run loose on your Moons, it's only a matter of time before you're hunted down.

This is what is known as "suicide by Moon." The lycanthrope basically just allows himself to run wild, knowing full well that he stands a good chance of getting killed before sunrise.

LETTING THE WOLF DEFINE THE MAN

There are some instances after a kill where you won't try to rationalize that getting loose is inevitable. You'll continue to restrain yourself at every Moon and will even take more precautions as the result of the mishap.

Instead, the darkness will creep into your day-to-day, dormant life.

Your demeanor might grow colder and more brusque. You will be far less patient with family and friends, possibly becoming abusive with your spouse or children. You might experience an increased propensity for cruelty to animals. You might even take pleasure in the misery of others, reaping enjoyment from the sight of the homeless or in response to footage of Third-World poverty or refugee camps. Ultimately, you will lose all compassion for other living things.

Just going through the motions of being a responsible lyc isn't enough. In this case, you are burying your emotional response to the kill, and those monstrous feelings are bubbling up into your day-to-day life, effectively turning you into a monster. If you go without confronting these feelings long enough, you can develop a

> **SIGNS THAT A LYCANTHROPE IS HEADING DOWN THE PATH TO DARKNESS**
> 1. Sudden embrace of religious extremism
> 2. Withdrawal from work or recreation activities
> 3. Growing acrimony with friends and loved ones
> 4. Cruelty toward animals
> 5. Abusiveness at home
> 6. Depression
> 7. Vague warnings about coming bloodshed
> 8. Dwindling bank accounts
> 9. Lapse in scheduled safehouse maintenance
> 10. Increased apathy
> 11. Lapse in hygiene
> 12. Failure to restrain "wolfouts" (peeing on things, howling in conversation, etc.)

psychosis and actually become dangerous in your dormant state, even though you continue to safeguard the populous from your werewolf form.

JUST FORGIVE

Accepting that you're a monster can be easier than accepting that you're a human being who's trying his best. Monsters don't have to struggle with guilt. The thing to remember, though, is that there have been a whole lot of monsters throughout history who were fully human. They just made a choice to shed their humanity and commit monstrous acts. You're making a choice too.

THE ARGUMENT FOR LYCANTHROPE ASCENDANCE

Some lycanthropes believe it is wrong to hide who they are. They feel that lycanthropy is as natural as humanity, and they should be no more expected to hide their nature than should humans. Lycanthrope Ascendance is a movement to encourage lycanthropes to come out of hiding and force the human population to accept the werewolf reality. We reprint below a letter from a proponent of Lycanthrope Ascendance who has had a great deal of correspondence with us and has made it very clear that he believes this book is doing lycanthropes a great disservice:

> Dear Editors,
> I write to you today to implore you to please abandon your undertaking, as the central message of your "manual" does nothing but harm to lycanthropes present and future. Encouraging werewolves to keep their identities hidden only

Sometimes solidarity can be a very bad thing

reinforces the notion that lycanthropy is the stuff of legend or the occult.

You claim to seek above all to help lycanthropes stay alive, and yet you encourage them to relegate themselves into a position where the burden of a non-lyc's protection from the lycanthrope is solely on the shoulders of the ly-canthrope. This in essence gives non-lycs a free pass to kill lycanthropes if they get loose.

Why not encourage werewolf awareness amongst all hu-mans, rather than werewolf secrecy amongst lycanthropes? If they realize we are here and we aren't going away, they can begin to accept it.

If you insist on going forward with your book, I ask that you include this note in its entirety so that lycanthropes can know that they are deserving of the same freedoms as the rest of humanity. And that one day society will have no choice but to accept us and protect themselves from us, which is obviously their responsibility, just as it is the responsibility of every prey to protect itself from the predator.

Signed,

XXXXXX XXXXXXXXX

The author's name was withheld, despite his insistence that we print it.

We include this letter out of respect for the belief, held passionately by some, that it is wrong to encourage lycanthropes to remain hidden. Though we respect the intent behind the Lycanthrope Ascendance movement, we simply find it extremely shortsighted and cannot in good conscience counsel lycanthropes to follow this road.

The central argument of Lycanthrope Ascendance is that werewolves have survived the natural selection process just as non-lycs have, and werewolves have just as much right to live on this earth as do non-lycs. Further, nowhere else in nature does the predator take precautions to protect its prey from itself, so non-lycs should be responsible for their own protection from werewolves. The Ascendance camp wants lycanthropes to organize and rise up in numbers to let the world know that there are far too many of them for non-lycs to wipe out.

We agree that lycanthropes being forced to keep their nature a secret is wrong. Unfortunately, we also believe it to be necessary.

If you give people the opportunity to realize they are prey and that there is a deadly predator in their midst, they will most definitely protect themselves. They will more than likely form armed mobs and go on werewolf hunts. To believe that society will simply adapt to a world where werewolves run free is pure folly. Does the ascendance community expect all of non-lyc society to lock itself away three nights out of the month so that the relatively small lycanthrope population can have their run of the land?

The fact is, a lycanthrope's prey *is* capable of defending itself. Even against the mighty werewolf. Non-lycs can shoot guns. They can mow you down with cars. They can find you in your home on a non-Moon day when you're as vulnerable as they are, and they can string you up from a lamppost. Lycanthropes have met such fates far too many times to count.

Famous Lycs Through Time
Rosa Parks, Civil Rights Activist
(1913–2005,
Lyc yrs: 2003–2005)
Was bitten very late in life. Despite persistent efforts to recruit her, she refused to lend her celebrity to the Lycanthrope Ascendance movement.

We maintain that our main purpose is to help lycanthropes stay alive and to enjoy full, happy lives. We see no way for this to be possible that does not involve secrecy. We don't think this is the way things should be. We are simply helping lycanthropes adapt to the way things are.

It's Not a Death Sentence

You've reached the office of Dr. Lauren Storms. I will be unreachable until the fifteenth of November. If this is an emergency, press star-89 to be immediately connected to the office of Dr. Morton Levy, who has graciously agreed to handle emergencies. Otherwise, feel free to leave a message, and I will get back to you promptly when I return. Have a wonderful day.

—Outgoing voicemail message recorded on November 12, 2008, one day before the full moon. A well-adjusted professional who has mastered living with lycanthropy, Dr. Storms records a similar message every month.

Well, first off, congratulations. You've (almost) gotten through this entire book. On behalf of the community of peaceful, well-adjusted lycanthropes, their families, friends, and loved ones, as well as the vast majority of non-lyc society who continue to labor under the blissful illusion that werewolves do not walk among them, we thank you. By learning the lessons in this book, implementing them in your lives, and passing them on to either your pureblood lycanthropic children or any newly bitten werewolves whose paths you cross, you have helped to save a tremendous amount of lives.

A lot of people, both lycanthropes and non-lycs alike, have contributed to this book, and we thank all of them for their hard work, their sacrifices, their courage, and their desire to help create a workable blueprint for living with lycanthropy. We thank them for talking to us, and we thank those who are no longer with us for writing it down. In the twenty-first century, we see a future for werewolves that includes fewer pitchfork wielding mobs and more masters degrees, flexible work schedules, loving families, and secure safe rooms. You can do much more than simply survive with this condition—you can thrive.

You can honor the struggles of those who came before you simply by staying alive and keeping safe. It is our hope that the publication of this manual will lead to a bright new day for the survival rate of Stage 1 lycanthropes, but the guidance contained within these pages is far from the last word. With every recently bitten werewolf who figures out a way to make it through his early Moons alive and murder-free, another chapter is ready to go to print. With a larger, more informed lycanthropic community will come new techniques, new coping mechanisms, but also new dangers. The future will surely bring new breeds of werewolf hunters, new weapons developed to track and murder your kind, and God forbid, you may even witness in your lifetime the resurgence of another government program like the Düsseldorf Project. You're in the fight now, and we can't have you on the sidelines. Being bitten is just the beginning.

Thanks to your knowledge, you are now a holder of the torch, and it is up to you to keep it burning and to pass it on. You have been given a wonderful and powerful gift, and you shouldn't be afraid to live life to the fullest. Sure, you need to stick to a fairly strict schedule these days, but so do the parents of a new infant. There are lots of people today whose quality of life is directly dependent on following a specific schedule of care and treatment, but for all the sacrifices they endure, few of them have the ability to rip the head off a live ox. So go ahead and live a little!

But most importantly, take it one day at a time and don't let yourself get too down. No matter how rough it gets, don't ever think that just because you transform into a beast three nights out of the month, your life as you know it has to end. Think about it: How can something that adds years to your life can ever be considered a death sentence?

Is being a werewolf the worst thing in the world? Absolutely not. In fact, just for a second, take the whole scary "werewolf" part out of it. Yes, that's a pretty big part, but just for a moment, take those three days a month, thirty-six days a year, out of the equation. Now think about what you are being given for the rest of those 329 days. Three hundred and twenty-nine days! That's a heck of a lot of time every year that you have absolute, 100 percent control over. Plus, you are stronger, faster, and healthier than almost every other person on the planet, and your sensory experience of the world makes you feel as though you've just taken a euphoric drug (without the hangover). If there were some kind of a pill or cream that could allow people to see without their glasses, smell an incredible layering of scents from miles away, and become strong, healthy, and coordinated without strenuous exercise, it would be the biggest seller in the history of the pharmaceutical industry. And you just got yourself a lifetime prescription, totally free of charge!

Now put the werewolf part back in. It's scary, sure, but if you must endure the ordeal of your Moons (and let's face it, you must), all you have to do is prepare for it. Once that work is done, you are free as a bird. Reach out with all of your senses to truly enjoy the upside of your wonderfully enhanced lifestyle to come. If nothing else, your life will definitely be an adventure.

So get out there and live it!

Acknowledgments

Ritch wants to thank his wife, Rachel.

Bob wants to thank his wife, Amanda.

Bob and Ritch want to thank Byrd Leavell for keeping the whole thing moving, Becky Cole for getting it all started, and Hallie Falquet for bringing it into the finish. Extra-special thanks to Emily Flake for churning out a giant pile of the most beautiful illustrations of gore, harnesses, and other snapshots from the lycanthrope lifestyle. For providing support, guidance, and expert counsel, thanks to Bob Duncan, Sean Hooley, Kevin Maher, Dr. Elizabeth Rice Smith, Dr. John Gullett, Kirk Thompson, The Lindsay Milligan Society, and Jefferson St. Leather and Bondage in Springton.

This book could not have been written without participation from the brave and selfless lycanthropes who lent their wisdom and insight so that future werewolves might have a better life. Their contribution to lycanthrope life is immeasurable. Thank you.

Appendix

TRANSFORMATION DATES:
2009–11

The following tables provide every lycanthrope's dates of transformation between the years 2009 and 2011. You will transform into a werewolf on the evening before the full moon, the evening of the full moon, and the evening following the full moon of each and every month. These three transformations are known as the werewolf's "Moon Set." The schedule of moons listed here uses Greenwich Mean Time (GMT). For more information, or if you are picking up this book after December 2011, refer to Chapter 6, "When It Will Happen and What It Will Feel Like."

Warning: Always double-check your dates using a local source. Very occasionally, full moons can appear on different days in different time zones. While this is very rare, it is absolutely crucial that you get your transformation dates correct.

2009	First Transformation	Second Transformation	Third Transformation
January 2009	Saturday, January 10	Sunday, January 11	Monday, January 12
February 2009	Sunday, February 8	Monday, February 9	Tuesday, February 10
March 2009	Tuesday, March 10	Wednesday, March 11	Thursday, March 12
April 2009	Wednesday, April 8	Thursday, April 9	Friday, April 10
May 2009	Friday, May 8	Saturday, May 9	Sunday, May 10
June 2009	Saturday, June 6	Sunday, June 7	Monday, June 8
July 2009	Monday, July 6	Tuesday, July 7	Wednesday, July 8
August 2009	Wednesday, August 5	Thursday, August 6	Friday, August 7
September 2009	Thursday, September 3	Friday, September 4	Saturday, September 5
October 2009	Saturday, October 3	Sunday, October 4	Monday, October 5
November 2009	Sunday, November 1	Monday, November 2	Tuesday, November 3
December 2009	Tuesday, December 1	Wednesday, December 2	Thursday, December 3
December 2009–January 2010	Wednesday, December 30	Thursday, December 31	Friday, January 1, 2010

NOTE: The third moon of the Moon Set beginning on December 30, 2009, takes place on the January 1, 2010. Please make note of this overlap.

2010	First Transformation	Second Transformation	Third Transformation
January 2010	Friday, January 29	Saturday, January 30	Sunday, January 31
February–			
March 2010	Saturday February 27	Sunday, February 28	Monday, March 1
March 2010	Monday, March 29	Tuesday, March 30	Wednesday March 31
April 2010	Tuesday, April 27	Wednesday, April 28	Thursday, April 29
May 2010	Wednesday, May 26	Thursday, May 27	Friday, May 28
June 2010	Friday, June 25	Saturday, June 26	Sunday, June 27
July 2010	Sunday, July 25	Monday, July 26	Tuesday, July 27
August 2010	Monday, August 23	Tuesday, August 24	Wednesday, August 25
September 2010	Wednesday, September 22	Thursday, September 23	Friday, September 24
October 2010	Friday, October 22	Saturday, October 23	Sunday, October 24
November 2010	Saturday, November 20	Sunday, November 21	Monday, November 22
December 2010	Monday, December 20	Tuesday, December 21	Wednesday, December 22

2011	First Transformation	Second Transformation	Third Transformation
January 2011	Tuesday, January 18	Wednesday, January 19	Thursday, January 20
February 2011	Thursday, February 17	Friday, February 18	Saturday, February 19
March 2011	Friday, March 18	Saturday, March 19	Sunday, March 20
April 2011	Sunday, April 17	Monday, April 18	Tuesday, April 19
May 2011	Monday, May 16	Tuesday, May 17	Wednesday, May 18
June 2011	Tuesday, June 14	Wednesday, June 15	Thursday, June 16
July 2011	Thursday, July 14	Friday, July 15	Saturday, July 16
August 2011	Friday, August 12	Saturday, August 13	Sunday, August 14
September 2011	Sunday, September 11	Monday, September 12	Tuesday, September 13
October 2011	Tuesday, October 11	Wednesday, October 12	Thursday, October 13
November 2011	Wednesday, November 9	Thursday, November 10	Friday, November 11
December 2011	Friday, December 9	Saturday, December 10	Sunday, December 11

ABOUT THE AUTHORS

RITCH DUNCAN AND BOB POWERS have devoted their lives to aiding and serving the lycanthrope community. They live in New York City.

EMILY FLAKE is a New York–based cartoonist and illustrator who is grateful to have gotten close enough to study her subjects for this book without being torn limb from limb.